MY DISCOVERY OF AMERICA

Books by Farley Mowat

People of the Deer
The Regiment
Lost in the Barrens
The Dog Who Wouldn't Be
Grey Seas Under
The Desperate People
Owls in the Family
The Serpent's Coil
The Black Joke
Never Cry Wolf
Westviking
The Curse of the Viking Grave
Canada North
This Rock Within the Sea (with John de Visser)
The Boat Who Wouldn't Float
The Siberians
A Whale for the Killing
Wake of the Great Sealers (with David Blackwood)
The Snow Walker
The Great Betrayal: Arctic Canada Now
And No Birds Sang: One Man's War
The World of Farley Mowat (*edited by Peter Davison*)
Sea of Slaughter
My Discovery of America

Edited by Farley Mowat
Coppermine Journey
Ordeal by Ice
The Polar Passion

MY DISCOVERY OF
AMERICA

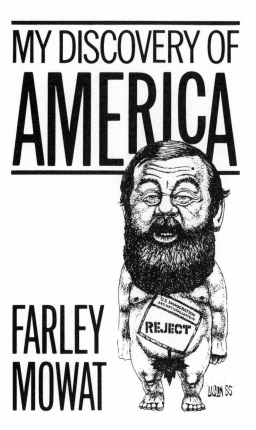

FARLEY
MOWAT

The Atlantic Monthly Press
Boston/New York

American First Edition

ISBN 0-87113-050-5

Printed in Canada

Contents

Foreword/7

Prologue/9

I Tuesday, April 23/13

II Wednesday, April 24/28

III Thursday, April 25/48

IV Friday, April 26/63

V Saturday and Sunday, April 27 and 28/78

VI Monday and Tuesday, April 29 and 30/88

VII Wednesday to Friday, May 1-3/103

VIII Saturday, May 4/117

A Postscript/123

Foreword

For most of my sixty-four years, I have lived close to the "world's longest undefended border" – the imaginary line dividing Canada from the United States of America. Nine out of ten Canadians live within a hundred miles or so of this boundary, which, they fondly believe, is little more than a property line between two especially good neighbours.

Throughout much of my life, I, too, believed this to be the case, having been a frequent visitor in my neighbour's yard. On the first occasion, I was still in my mother's womb and, had she delayed in Cleveland a few more weeks, I might have first seen the light of day in the U.S.A. – and been able to claim dual citizenship in consequence.

I travelled back and forth many times before reaching puberty, and have done so often enough since, usually in connection with my work as a writer but sometimes simply for the fun of it. In the course of these travels, I have gone from Atlantic to Pacific, and from the northern tier of states south into Mexico.

I thought I knew the place.

The chasm of my ignorance began to gape before me on Tuesday, April 23, 1985. This book is an account of what ensued thereafter.

Although in one sense it is about me, in a much larger and more important sense I play only a walk-through part in a story that is more concerned with how *other* people saw and reacted to the circumstances in which I found myself enmeshed. It is perhaps best categorized as a case history. As such, it consists largely of the observations, deductions, conclusions, and opinions of others.

I cannot begin to acknowledge all of these people by name since the roster includes not only scores of reporters, editorial and other writers, and interviewers, but also hundreds of individuals who, in addition to their letters, sent me a mountain of newspaper and magazine clippings, together with much other information that would not otherwise have come my way. Some of them I cannot name in any case, since they made their contributions in confidence.

Nevertheless, to one and all, I give my abiding gratitude. I acknowledge that this is *your* book as much as mine, and I hope it carries the message that almost all of you were so anxious to express in your separate and distinctive ways.

I must make one additional acknowledgment: I am grateful to the Immigration and Naturalization Service of the U.S. Department of Justice, without which this book could not have been written.

Prologue

Michael Bauman, Professor of English, and a prime mover in the Canadian Studies faculty of California State University at Chico, began it all.

Where is Chico? Well may you ask. I've learned it lies a couple of hours' drive north of Sacramento, California, under the loom of the Sierra Nevada Mountains. I think it is a small agricultural town. It is where Michael Bauman lives.

Three or four years ago, Michael got a bee in his bonnet. He decided to persuade a Canadian writer, namely me, to visit Chico, give a seminar or two, and talk about his work, his hopes, his dreams. Michael decided to do this because he liked my books and because he thought I would be a good person to help dispel the myth of the Great White North.

This is a delusion afflicting many Americans, one that makes them shiver apprehensively on those rare occasions when they acknowledge the existence of a frozen wasteland lying mainly to the north of the 49th parallel of latitude, inhabited by a meagre scattering of beer-drinking, parka-clad, bacon-eating lumberjacks, polar bears, and scarlet-coated stalwarts of the Royal Canadian Mounted Police.

Michael wrote to me. He wrote and he wrote. I ignored the first several letters but, eventually, impressed by his persistence, I replied, telling him there was no way under God I was going to travel all the way to Chico, wherever that might be, to bend the ears of his students. When he nevertheless continued to importune me, I lied. I said: Well, maybe I could come *next* year; why not ask me then?

When the next year came, he asked me. By then, he had begun to intrigue me, as had his Canadian Studies faculty. In Chico, California? Such faculties are extremely rare in the United States and the few about which I have previously

9

heard all nestle under the wings of major eastern universities. So, finally, in the autumn of 1984, I responded to the current Bauman plea by opining that I might consider a visit the following spring, if a way could be found to fund the expedition.

Michael found a way. He besieged Canadian Consulate officials in San Francisco, pleading with them to get Mowat for him. Since it so happened that the Canadian Consulates in Los Angeles, San Francisco, and Seattle had all received requests to bring me to the West Coast to talk to students, literary clubs, and environmental groups, his plea fell on fertile ground.

In January, 1985, the cultural director of the Department of External Affairs (Canada's State Department, as it were) asked me to undertake a tour of the American West Coast. Since my current book, *Sea of Slaughter*, was to be published in the United States late in April, I agreed to go then, providing I could combine promotion of the book with my duties as a cultural emissary. External Affairs readily concurred, and commissioned the Writers' Union of Canada to arrange the details of my itinerary and travel plans.

Michael was now well on the way to achieving his purpose. While he was busily engaged making preparations for my arrival in Chico, my wife and I flew to Australia for the month of March, where I attended a writers' conference, then lectured at a number of universities, all under the aegis of External Affairs, at the invitation of Edward Schreyer, Canadian High Commissioner (a synonym for Ambassador) to Australia.

We had barely arrived home at the end of March when Bauman called me. He was distraught, and he was mad. Did *I* know that External Affairs had cancelled out? I did not know. I phoned the Writers' Union and the news was confirmed. "All three consulates," I was told, "seem to have simultaneously discovered they are going to be too busy to receive you. They suggest a postponement, but are vague as to future dates."

I called Michael back and apologized on behalf of my government and myself; but, in all honesty, I was somewhat relieved. In truth, I had had quite enough of travel for the nonce and was looking forward to some peace and quiet at home. In hoping for such, I did not reckon with the indomitable Mr. Bauman.

During my absence in Australia he had been in close touch with the lady at the Writers' Union who was arranging my itinerary, and both had been collaborating with my American publishers, Atlantic Monthly Press of Boston and New York. When External Affairs so abruptly dropped the project, my publishers decided to go it alone, much applauded by Michael Bauman. "We were having nothing but trouble getting straight answers from the staff in your consulates anyway," I was told. "You, and we, are probably better off without them."

I was not so sure. A new and much heavier itinerary had been arranged – one intended to promote my book to the saturation point. But Chico had not been forgotten. I was to spend an uncluttered weekend there as the house guest of the Baumans, and it was this happy prospect that persuaded me to accept the new ordeal.

So as you can see, ultimate responsibility for all that subsequently came to pass must be laid squarely at Michael Bauman's door.

Reproduced courtesy Terry Mosher.

I

Tuesday, April 23

Depart Pearson International Airport, Toronto, 1:15 p.m.
Air Canada Flight #795.
 Arrive Los Angeles, 3:30 p.m.
 You will be met by a Prime Time Limo and taken to your
hotel, the Beverly Wilshire.

"Promotion tours," I complained to my wife, Claire, as I
dragged my suitcase to the front door, "are a royal pain in the
ass. Don't know why I let myself get suckered into them. Jet
lag in a dozen cities that all look and smell alike – rat-racing
from radio studio to TV studio to do the same damn interview
for the umpteenth time – autographing 'parties' where the
only body that turns up is a fifth cousin, twice removed!"

"Think of the bright side," Claire said soothingly. "The
adulation; the free booze; the swish hotel suites; the chance
to twirl your kilt in public . . . Besides, how else can we
writers get the kind of publicity we need to sell our books?"

"I'll think about that," I grumbled, sliding into the passen-
ger seat beside neighbour David Brooks, who was driving me
to the airport. "Meanwhile, take care, honey. See you in ten
days' time . . . if I survive."

It was a magnificent spring morning, bright, warm, and
tranquil, as we drove out of Port Hope, the little town on the
north shore of Lake Ontario where I spend part of my year.
David thought so, too.

"Nice day for a trip," he offered.

"Nicer day to stay home and plant the bleeding garden!" I
snapped.

Sensing my mood, he said no more as we made the seventy-
five-mile freeway trek to Toronto's Malton Airport – now

pompously renamed Lester B. Pearson International in honour of a defunct Prime Minister.

But David was right. It *was* a charming day. And, despite myself, I began to feel little twinges of excitement, even anticipation, at the prospect of visiting the West Coast of the United States: Los Angeles, San Francisco, Sacramento and the little university town of Chico, then finally Seattle. Some of it was bound to be worthwhile, even if I did have to spend most of my time peddling my book, which had, by no mere coincidence, been published that very day in the United States.

Over the years I had received hundreds of good letters from Californians and Washingtonians who had read my earlier books. And Peter Davison, friend and editor of three decades' standing at Atlantic, had called to cheer me on.

"You'll find it stimulating. The West Coast has the worst, and some of the best of America to offer. Furthermore, people there *buy books* . . . and even read them."

Ah, well, I thought, as we pulled into the airport. It may not be so bad. After all, I *was* being sent First Class – a condition that makes air travel almost tolerable. In deference to this munificence on the part of my publishers, I had dressed soberly in a pair of impeccably creased grey slacks, a tweedy jacket, and something I almost never wear – a tie.

David bade me farewell and departed. Feeling quite chipper now, I made my way through the vast terminal building to an enclave occupied by U.S. Customs and Immigration. I presented myself to the Customs counter.

Having first determined where I was bound, a sallow fellow with a long-suffering face asked if I had anything to declare.

"Nothing but good intentions," I replied cheerfully, if stupidly.

He winced. "Open the bag!"

I did so and he rumpled aimlessly through it; but when he came to my kilt in all its yards of gaudy tartan, he stopped, raised his pale eyes to mine, and said accusingly:

"This is a *skirt*!"

"No," I explained. "It is a kilt."

"You wear that thing?"

"I do indeed. And proudly."

"A *skirt*," he reiterated. " 'Frisco ought to suit you good."

A trifle less jauntily, I moved on to a sort of toll booth presided over by a uniformed young man whose shoulder flashes proclaimed him to be a member of the INS – the Immigration and Naturalization Service of the United States of America. He was wispy, sandy-haired, bespectacled, and mild of manner. I warmed to him at once. Here, surely, was the archetypal, shy, but friendly American.

He asked me the usual routine questions, accepting all my answers with a nod . . . until he came to the purpose of my journey.

"Business," I told him. And then I breached what fellow-author Max Braithwaite calls the cardinal rule for dealing with customs and immigration officials the world over. *Never Volunteer Information!*

"I'm off to the West Coast to promote my newest book. I'm an author, you see."

His head came up and his eyes, behind their windows, seemed to sharpen. Vaingloriously, I thought he might have recognized me.

"Show me your tickets."

I passed them over.

"Your name is Mao-it?"

"*Mo*wat – as in poet," I corrected him.

"So. Your first name Fairley?"

"*Far*ley," I said kindly. "As in barley." Since only my initials appeared on the airline tickets, I deduced from this exchange that he must know me by repute even if he couldn't pronounce my name. At any rate, he stamped my boarding pass and waved me into the corridor leading to the departure lounge.

I found a seat, got out a pocketbook, and prepared to read until the boarding call. But after five minutes or so, I became aware that the sandy-haired INS man had materialized beside me. He must have approached as softly as a cat.

"Ah ha," thought I smugly. "I'll bet he wants an autograph." I was actually reaching for my pen when he asked me to return to the immigration section. His tone was soft, but it was an order nonetheless. Nonplussed, I followed him to a tiny cubicle equipped only with a desk and one chair, which he pre-empted. Then, as I stood in increasing bewilderment before him, he peppered me with questions that carried a penetrating chill of menace.

"Have you ever been turned back at the U.S. border?"

"Never!"

"Have you entered, or attempted to enter the U.S.A. illegally?"

"Of course not!"

"Do you have a criminal record?"

"Certainly not!"

"Is there a security file on you in the U.S.A.?"

"Now how would I know that?"

The impertinence of these questions was beginning to annoy me. "What the devil's going on? You already passed me through – remember?"

"I need further identification."

"Well," thought I. "They must be confusing me with someone else. Thank God I've brought my passport." Although neither passport nor visa is usually required of Canadians visiting the United States, I invariably carry that magic little book whenever I go abroad. With something of a flourish I produced it.

The INS man flipped it open, stared at the rogues' gallery portrait contained therein, then without a word stood up and ambled off, the passport in his hand.

"Excuse me," I asked of his retreating back. "Should I wait here or in the departure lounge?"

"Wait there," he replied, without even deigning to turn his head.

Indignant at his rudeness, but baffled and bewildered, too, my thoughts raced. What was happening here? It had to be some minor bureaucratic muddle! There could be no earthly reason the Americans, in this, the sixty-fourth year of my life, should decide to keep me out! Probably a case of mistaken identity. But if that sandy-haired gumshoe didn't hurry back, I might miss my flight.

Ten – fifteen minutes dragged by. Flight time was inexorably approaching and I have a life-long fear of missing planes and trains. Anxiously I peered down the long hallway and at last saw my man approaching.

He took his time. Once he stopped to exchange badinage with a female clerk. Once he turned back, as if he had forgotten something, then again reversed himself. But as he finally reached the cubicle, I saw there was a faint smile on his face.

My relief was monumental. I was so pleased to think that the *contretemps*, whatever it might have been about, had been resolved that I returned the pale one's smile with a broad and grateful grin. I held out my hand for my passport, and was about to hasten to the departure lounge where boarding was just beginning, when the INS man dropped his bombshell.

"You are excluded from entering the United States."

He issued this stunning dictum with a righteousness that would have suited St. Peter turning a poor sinner away from the Pearly Gates.

"I *what*?"

"You are not permitted to enter the United States of America." He was being patient now but, I suspect, enjoying himself.

I, most assuredly, was neither.

"Why in blazes can't I?"

"I can't tell you that."

"You *know*, but you bloody well won't tell me?"

"You could say that."

"*I* could say that! Who *will* tell me? What in Christ's sweet name is going *on* here? And what the hell am I supposed to do about it?"

I think I may have raised my voice a trifle. A few passengers being "processed" in other booths craned their necks in our direction. Gumshoe picked up a fragment of paper and pencilled two telephone numbers on it – just the numbers, nothing else.

"You could call these," he said, in a tone that suggested the uselessness of such an exercise.

Furiously I snatched the paper and scanned it, noting that the area codes were unfamiliar and therefore doubtless too distant to be of any immediate assistance – even had he volunteered the use of a telephone, which he did not. In order to call these anonymous numbers, I would have to go and find a pay phone in the main terminal; *but there was no time.* There was barely time, I realized distractedly, to rescue my bag and my precious kilt. It was already too late to rescue my *sang-froid.*

"Piss on you!" I flung at my sandy-haired nemesis, and ran for the baggage area. First things first.

A few moments later, a black Customs employee was listening sympathetically to my incoherent story. He shook his head sadly.

"Your bag's already left for L.A. I'm sorry. But don't worry. They'll put it on the first plane back to Toronto."

He noted the particulars and went off to send a retrieval telex to Los Angeles, and it was only then that I began to comprehend fully the incontestable reality – *I was not going on my journey to Los Angeles!*

Panic and confusion filled my thoughts. "What about my airline and hotel reservations?" was the first, inane reaction. Then, "Mother of God! What about all the people awaiting my arrival? . . . publishers' representatives, media people, TV producers, book sellers, book *buyers* . . . who would straighten *that* mess out?

"And what about Susan DiSesa in Atlantic's New York office, who had sweated blood to make the publicity arrangements for the tour? . . . And Peter Davison in Boston? . . . and Michael Bauman in Chico? . . .

"And what about me, for God's sake?" Having been stopped from entering the United States by contemptuous officialdom, and without being offered a shred of explanation, I was actually feeling *guilty*, as if I was some wetback who had been caught trying to crash the border! "Why should *I* be feeling guilty? And why . . . why had they *done* this to me anyway?"

Confused, outraged, and growing angrier by the second, I knew I needed help. I made a mad dash for the nearest exit.

Outside, in the bright April sunshine, I swerved unseeingly toward what I took to be a taxi, flung myself inside, and snarled the address of my Toronto publishers.

Only then did I realize I was in no ordinary cab. This vehicle was an obscenely-stretched limousine, equipped with one-way windows, a bar, TV, and a curved divan upholstered in mauve velvet. It was the sort of harem buggy one associates with Hollywood celebrities, and a phrase from my tour schedule flashed before my eyes . . . *You will be met by a Prime Time Limo and driven to the Beverly Wilshire . . .*

The faceless, factory-like premises of McClelland and Stewart can have nothing in common with the *Beverly Wilshire*, and my limo created something of a sensation when it drew up at the front door.

"I thought it must belong to either the Premier of Ontario, or the Mafia," the receptionist told me. She also told me that Jack McClelland, chairman of the company, to whose comforting arms I was fleeing, had not come in this day from his country home. However, his executive assistant, Marge Hodgeman, was in her office.

Marge was astonished to see me. When I explained as best I could what had happened, fire flew from her eyes. Marge is nothing if not loyal.

"How could they dare!" she cried. "The little wimps! Wait 'til Jack hears this. I'll ring him right away. But first you need a drink. Hang on, I'll get you one."

Jack was equally astonished – then magnificently blasphemous.

"So what do you plan to do now?" he asked when he had run down.

"I don't really know. I guess I have to call New York and Boston and break the news. Then, well, I guess I'll catch the afternoon train back to Port Hope. Surprise the devil out of Claire! I really don't think there's any way the Yanks are going to let me make the trip. To tell the truth, Jack, there is no goddamn way I *want* to make it, after what I've just been through. Screw the lot of them! Maybe Claire and I'll go to the cottage for a couple of days and look at birds."

Jack was appalled. "You'll do no such bloody thing! My God, Farley, don't you realize what's happened here? Canada's foremost writer *proposing to slink away like a whipped cur because Uncle Sam lays one on him? And,*" he snorted like an angry horse, "go off and look at effing *birds*?"

Words temporarily failed him. Then:

"Listen, man. Let Peter know. Then have Marge call you a cab and get yourself out here. We are going to have a council of war. We are going to make those idiots wish they'd never heard your name. The media will go ape over this one . . . Mowat barred from the U-S-of-A while Prime Minister Mulroney is trumpeting to the wide world how lovey-dovey we and the Yankees are. Oh, they love us down in Washington all right! *You be here in an hour's time.*"

This was vintage McClelland. Commander of a motor torpedo boat during the war, Jack has never lost his lust for combat, especially against heavy odds. As I polished off my drink, it struck me that Mowat and McClelland against the Empire of the Reagan Eagle *was* pretty heavy odds. I downed another drink. But what the hell . . . Goddamn it, Jack was *right*!

I talked briefly to Claire, who was properly stunned by my news; and then Marge got Peter Davison on the line. He was frankly incredulous, refusing to believe my rejection could be anything more than a tempest in an airport, as it were.

"Calm yourself, Farley. I'll make a call to Washington. We'll get to the bottom of this idiocy. Susan will see if she can shuffle your appointments and get you on a later plane tonight."

"Peter, I think you're absolutely wrong. God alone knows why, but I got the impression the guardians of your fair land want no part of me."

As is his fashion, Peter raised his voice and overrode me.

"Nonsense, Farley. You are being irrational. This is just a simple error. I'll call Jack's place when we've cleared it up."

It took nearly an hour to drive from Toronto to McClelland's home near the village of Kleinberg – time for me to sort through some of the impressions and events and try to find some answers. One thing seemed clear – it would be a delusion to think that my exclusion had been a matter of mistaken identity. When the gumshoe went off with my passport, it could only have been to check with his superior in the flesh, or with that supreme superior, the computer. The result had been unequivocal. Farley McGill Mowat – he, himself, and no other – was *persona non grata* in the United States of America.

For whatever reason.

But what, indeed, could that reason be? Perhaps there was a clue in the questions gumshoe had fired at me. A criminal record? No – nothing there that I could think of. Turned back at the U.S. border? Perhaps someone *else* had been turned back, using my name? . . . but that was too far-fetched. How about illegal border crossings? None of that either . . . ah, but wait a moment . . .

In 1967, Claire and I had sailed our little schooner up the St. Lawrence seaway *en route* to Lake Ontario. Passing out of the seaway locks near Cornwall at dusk one day, we were smothered in dense fog and I instinctively did what I have always done in such situations – scuttled for the nearest port. This happened to be Massena, on the New York side of the river.

The schooner felt her way to an abandoned dock where I thankfully made fast for the night. What I did *not* do was hie me to the nearest U.S. Customs and Immigration post to report my entry. Worse still, I landed an illegal alien.

He (or it may have been she) had come aboard surreptitiously somewhere along the Gaspé coast and had been hiding in the chain-locker ever since. We knew about his presence mainly because of footsteps on deck during the night. But after we left Massena (at dawn next day, to avoid attracting official attention), we heard no more from him. He had jumped ship. He may have been a rat, or perhaps a weasel – or even a singularly heavy-footed meadow mouse. Grasping at straws, I wondered if this incident had been observed by some gimlet-eyed immigration snoop.

Or – and another shrouded memory was unfurled – there was the day in 1968 when, southbound in a chartered float-plane from Old Crow in Yukon Territory, my pilot lost his way in low cloud and we unwittingly strayed into Alaska. Clawing through mountain valleys almost at deck level, we eventually encountered a road. Knowing it had to be the Alaska Highway (there was no other in that region), we turned east and followed it at an altitude of about fifty feet until we were safely back in Canada. On this occasion we certainly *were* observed, for we passed so closely over the border post that I saw two uniformed officials duck for cover.

But, no again . . . even if the U.S. knew about these two incursions, they could hardly be sufficient grounds to bar me out.

Then what about the reference to a mysterious "security file"? I was still chewing on that one when my taxi pulled up at the McClelland home.

With the scent of coming battle flaring his nostrils, Jack welcomed me and led the way to his den. Little lights on his several telephones were flickering impatiently. A full bottle of vodka, together with glasses and ice, stood ready for action. Jack, as dashing and debonair as ever, waved me to a chair while he continued an interrupted phone conversation with the company solicitor.

"Sorry, Bob. Farley just arrived . . . You really think he could be on the blacklist? How the hell do we find out? Okay, let me know if you come up with anything."

Jack hung up.

"We may have a problem, Farley," he said thoughtfully. "Bob thinks you have probably been barred under something called the McCarran-Walter Act. You may have heard of it. Back in the 1950s, Joe McCarthy scared the U.S. Congress into passing a law that would exclude anyone, any time, on the mere suspicion of being a Commie or even a fellow traveller. Bob tells me that, under the law, the U.S. authorities don't even have to give reasons to the people they shaft. They don't even have to *have* a valid reason. Nevertheless, the impression that gets left with the public is that you are, or maybe were, a Commie. And there ain't *no* way to clear yourself."

"You've got to be joking!" I replied incredulously. "The Yanks got rid of all that fascist malarkey years ago!"

"I'm not joking. And they didn't. *And* if we make a stink about you being barred, and *they* claim they did it under the Commie clause of the McCarran Act, a lot of people could figure where there's smoke there must be fire; and that if U.S. Immigration claims you're Red, you likely are. It's dirty stuff, but it does what it was designed to do – scares the pants off anyone they finger. Makes the poor bastards lie down and play dead for fear of losing their reputations and their jobs; of seeing their friends and even their families turn against them. It's blackmail, man . . . and here's the pinch . . . are you prepared to take the chance of being clobbered if we go public? You never can tell for sure which way the media will jump."

This was definitely something to give me pause. The risk of being stigmatized as a Communist or a "com symp" by the U.S. government, and of subsequently being pilloried by right-wing elements in the United States and in my own country, was not attractive – especially not at a time when neoconservatism was in the ascendancy in both Canada and the U.S.A. The prospect of just quietly slipping off to the cottage to look at birds began to seem exceedingly attractive.

I temporized. It was then only about 4:00 p.m. and Peter Davison *might* be having some success. While we waited to hear from him, I could ring the two anonymous numbers given to me and, perhaps, make some small progress toward straightening out the situation myself.

"Right, then," said Jack. "Go ahead and make your calls. Meanwhile I know a guy at the Canadian Embassy in Washington and I'll see what he can tell us."

My first call was answered by the U.S. Customs and Immigration border post at the Rainbow Bridge, linking Niagara Falls, Ontario, with its namesake in New York State. The chap who answered seemed to be one of the duty officers whose task it is to check Canadian visitors entering the U.S.A. by car. He had never heard of me, nor did he seem to have any knowledge of my problem. He did offer to call me back after consulting his superiors. I never heard from him again.

The second number proved to be that of a U.S. Immigration office at Buffalo. Once again, the chap who answered apparently knew nothing about my case. "Hold on," he told me. "I'll get the superintendent on the line."

I waited five minutes, but nothing happened. Supposing that we had been disconnected, I hung up, then called again . . . with the same result, except that this time I waited nearly ten minutes for the elusive superintendent. Jack tried the third time; was told to wait; did so until his patience was exhausted; then slammed down the phone.

"They're giving you the goddamn run-around! Clearly nobody wants to talk to you. And my Embassy guy in Washington says he knows nothing about any problem with Farley Mowat, but says he's going to check it out with the INS brass. I'm going to try External Affairs in Ottawa, but don't hold your breath."

A light blinked for an incoming call and he motioned me to take it. A chastened Peter Davison was on the line.

"I'm afraid this really *is* a hell of a mess, Farley. We've talked to the Justice Department and they are not going to let you in. No reasons given. So we've had to tell Susan to begin cancelling your West Coast arrangements. What have you and Jack decided? Will you go to the press with this? Or do you want to let it drop?"

Jack had picked up the other handset. Now he cut in. "Peter? We are going to fight! We are going to blow the lid so goddamn high, it'll make a moon landing. Are you with us?"

"Oh, we're with you. Harry Evans, our new chief, is appalled, as I am, and he knows his way around in Washington and in the press, as former editor of the London *Times*. We'll start with the *New York Times*, the *Washington Post*, the *Boston Globe*, the *Los Angeles Times*, and go on from there. Good hunting on your side of the border."

Jack put the phone down and gave me his lopsided grin.

"Before you say anything, let *me* say this. You *have* to bite the bullet on this thing because, you see, it isn't just you; it's everyone who gets shit on this way by the Almighty Eagle. Consider it your *duty*, man . . . Now go and ask Elizabeth to cook some grub; then pour us both a drink. We've got a war to fight."

I sighed, but did as I was told. The die was cast.

We began our campaign with a string of calls alerting Canadian press services, then, through the good offices of Elsa Franklin, another stalwart friend, all major Canadian radio and television networks. Interest was immediate and electric. By 8:00 p.m., the story was on the national news on CBC, Global TV, and CTV. By 8:30, all the phones in the McClelland home were ringing off their hooks. Squeezed in among the media calls came a plaintive, somewhat desperate one from Claire.

"Farley, what on earth are you *doing*? The phone hasn't stopped for two solid hours. I can't get time to eat or even make a cup of tea. Some reporter just called from Vancouver and when he couldn't get you, tried to interview *me* on your so-called Communist history! *When*'ll you be *home*?"

I did not know, and had to tell her so.

Jack and I, together with his wife, Elizabeth, were now fielding a steady torrent of inquiries, all zeroing in on the same question: what, exactly, *had* Mowat done? As Paul Taylor of the *Globe and Mail* inelegantly put it: "Why *did* the Yanks give you the bum's rush?" He had already called the INS and had received no satisfaction from that source. As his published story said:

"U.S. Immigration officials are not telling Mr. Mowat or anyone else why they won't let him into their country . . . 'I can't give any information – nothing at all,' said Hyman Jackson, a U.S. Department of Immigration official in Buffalo, New York."

"They aren't *going* to say anything specific," Jack decided. "They'll just leave the implication hanging that you're a Commie baddie – one of the Kremlin's boys."

He seemed to be right, because there followed a number of forthright demands to know whether or not I was a Communist.

It was simple enough to tell the truth: that I was not and never had been either a Communist or a Communist sympathizer. It was not so easy to provide a credible alternative explanation. In some desperation I hazarded the guess that it might relate to an earlier book of mine, *Sibir* (*The Siberians* in the U.S.A.), an account of life in the Soviet far north based on two trips I made there in 1966 and 1969.

"That book treated the Soviets as human beings essentially like us," I explained to a reporter from the Associated Press. Although he did not seem entirely convinced that *Sibir* was the cause of my difficulties, he did agree that, given the current Evil Empire attitude of the Reagan administration, there might be something to it. Consequently, and for want of anything else to offer, it became my stock reply throughout the remainder of that hectic night.

Jack would not buy it. "That's old stuff, Farley, and there's no weight to it anyway. *I* think you're in trouble over

Sea of Slaughter. You've no idea how powerful the hunting lobby and the anti-environmental kooks are in Washington. And they will hate the book for the way you cut them up in it."

"Nonsense, Jack! Are you seriously telling me a lobby group like that could get a U.S. government department to shut the door on me?"

"Farley, be your age! And ask yourself, why *did* they turn you back? There *had* to be more to it than *Sibir*! That's fifteen years ago!"

We were interrupted by a call from a CBC story producer who had been independently pursuing the question of cause, although without success. However, he *had* tracked down the man nominally responsible for turning me away – one Benedict Ferro, District Director of the INS, in Buffalo.

"He takes full responsibility for stopping you, Mr. Mowat. At any rate, he's officially carrying the can. He says you were barred because of serious accusations against you which are contained in a file they have. He won't divulge the nature of them because he says that would intrude on your privacy rights; but an INS spokesman in Washington confirms they come under the McCarran-Walter Act. I have Mr. Ferro's home number if you'd like it."

Would we like it?

Peremptorily waving me aside, Jack dialed. He got through immediately.

"Mr. Ferro? Jack McClelland here. Farley Mowat's publisher. He'd like a word with you . . . You say the matter's so sensitive you'd rather *not* speak to him personally? Okay, I'm his representative. We'd like to know the charges against him. We'd like to know why he was given no explanation for being barred and what, in fact, that explanation is . . . You mean you *won't*? . . . I'm sorry, but you'd better realize this will be an international incident by morning and I hope you can find some believable explanations by then . . . Yes, I'll see that he gets that message."

Jack hung up and turned to me with a wry grin. "He won't talk to you, and he won't say why you were stopped; but it's obvious the media have already reached his bosses, and they'd clearly like to damp the story down. What he *does* say is that, if you come to the airport tomorrow morning, his people will, and I quote, 'review your file with you.' "

"Does that mean they'll let me in?"

"He didn't say. My guess is, it would depend on whether you'd be willing to let the whole thing drop, and even then, you might get the royal run-around."

"So what do you think we ought to do?"

"Tell them to go to hell! That you won't settle for anything less than full clearance and a public apology. I think they're beginning to realize they've got a tiger by the tail."

There was no doubt but that a tiger had broken loose that night. By 1:00 a.m., when we finally dropped into our beds, we had (according to Jack's telephone log) answered sixty-three media calls.

The question in my mind as I sought for sleep was could I ride this beast we had unleashed? Or would I end up in its gut?

Not by the hair on your chinney-chin-chin!

Reproduced courtesy *The Globe and Mail*, Toronto.

II

Wednesday, April 24

You will be picked up at your hotel at 9:30 a.m. by Bonnie Glass, your escort in the Los Angeles area. Your schedule includes:
"Something You Should Know", taped at KHTZ/KRLA
"Afternoon Break", Cable News Network
United Press International Audio interview
Associated Press broadcast interview
Los Angeles Times interview
Bookstore autographings as arranged

The sun streaming into the bedroom woke me early. Nobody else was up, so I made a pot of tea and took my cup out to the edge of an adjacent ravine whose trees were just beginning to bud.

Despite the solace offered by this lovely morning, I could not respond. There was a hollow feeling in the pit of my stomach; one not born of hunger. I was experiencing a sense of acute apprehension. What on earth, I asked myself once more, *had* I done to merit treatment of this kind? *Was* there, in fact, something buried below conscious memory that could justify it?

Down I dug into my own past. Perhaps my delinquency was connected with my sponsorship of the Fair Play for Cuba Committee away back in the early 1960s? Or what about my long-time and still-continuing association with the Campaign for Nuclear Disarmament, or Operation Dismantle, or Project Plowshare, or any of the other anti-war groups I supported? Maybe my sin was my endorsement of the radical ecological movement; or the fact that I had lent my name to the fund-raising efforts of the Coalition Against Acid

Rain, which was currently anathema in Washington? Or, maybe, I had been rejected as belated punishment for my anti-American stance during the Vietnam War . . .

A rapping on the kitchen window interrupted this bootless search for answers. Elizabeth beckoned, and I went in for breakfast.

"That was quite a night!" she said. "But the phone hasn't rung once this morning. Do you think it's run its course?" She sounded as if she were describing a fever.

"Let's hope!" I said fervently.

At which point the kitchen phone began to shrill. Elizabeth had not yet reached it before first one, then a second office phone began to ring. My heart sank. Jack, on his bedroom extension, could be heard roaring.

"The hell you say! We categorically deny it! If he's a Communist, then I'm the Pope in Rome!"

Tousle-haired, blue eyes popping with fury, he soon appeared at the kitchen door. "Coffee!" he demanded. "And where's the effing paper?" Elizabeth handed him the newspaper and he tore into it, suddenly stopped and began to read aloud:

"An enraged Farley Mowat vowed last night he will never return to the United States after he was denied entry to that country yesterday.

" 'I doubt I'll ever try to cross their goddamn border again. I won't put up with the indignity,' he bellowed from the home of publisher Jack McClelland where the pair were trying to unravel the mystery." . . . "Hmmm . . . hmmm, ah, *here* it is . . ."

"The author of 27 books can't get into the United States because U.S. officials suspect he holds views sympathetic with Communism.

" 'It has to do with his character,' revealed a senior U.S. immigration official, who asked not to be named. 'He could be a little pink.'

The District Director of the U.S. immigration department in Buffalo refused to disclose details of the Mowat case.

" 'I'm not free to discuss with you the factors that would violate his privacy or that of the U.S. government's case,' said Benedict Ferro . . . Ferro told Canadian Press that officials keep a list of individuals who are believed to be ineligible for entry . . . U.S. officials can refuse a person entry to the country for violating any one of 33 statutes, Ferro said. The statutes prohibit persons with criminal records and those holding Communist beliefs from entering the U.S., he said."

Jack flung down the paper. "They're really trying to *do* it!" he shouted. "Knock you out of the ring with the old Commie smear! The sons of bitches! There's an effing big rat in the warrens in Washington and by God, we are going to smoke him out!"

My choler had also risen sharply as I listened to the story, which already was, or soon would be, in every major newspaper across Canada. If this was to be war with no quarter given, then so be it.

"No quarter!" I muttered fiercely as I eyed the eggs Elizabeth had set before me.

"You don't *need* a quarter, man," said Jack distractedly. "There are five johns in this house, for God's sake, and all of them are free. Now let's get on with it. Yesterday was just a skirmish. Today we send in the massed battalions! Elizabeth, route all calls back to the office, but first, phone Marge and have her send the staff to battle stations. Farley! Ten minutes to down your grub, then we're away!"

It was close on 9:30 a.m. when Jack's Mustang varoomed out of the drive. I might have felt more secure with the unknown Bonnie Glass, even on the Los Angeles freeways, but as Jack veered through the late morning traffic, twiddling the radio dials as he tried to pick up the latest reports on the border incident, I was preoccupied by thoughts of what lay ahead.

First I had to come to grips with the fact that this was *my* war, not Jack's or Peter's, no matter how engaged they might become. It would have to be fought my way and I would have to lead the charge. I was now sufficiently infuriated by the innuendo tactics American officialdom was employing against me to go all out. But what tactics should *I* use? I knew the answer even before I asked myself the question.

Since volunteering to go and fight the Nazis in World War II (I served nearly four years with the Canadian Army, much of that time in action with the infantry), I have frequently found myself on collision course with the kind of establishment *fonctionnaires* whom I collectively epitomize as "cementheads." These are the often arrogant and always insensitive automatons who populate far too many echelons of every nation's political, economic, military, and even religious structures. They are anathema to me – a contradiction of what humanity is, or should be, all about.

And long ago – in self-defence – I discovered how best to deal with them. The most effective weapons are simply: ridicule and mockery.

As Jack wheeled into the McClelland and Stewart parking lot and braked abruptly, I turned to him.

"Hold it a minute, Jack. You've been terrific, and you know how grateful I am. But what happens from here on in has to do with *my* neck. I have to do it my way – but not to worry, I'll do it up brown!"

Jack grinned. His right hand came up in a mocking naval salute. "Senior service at your service, *Sir*! Let's go and give 'em shit!"

Marge Hodgeman had done her stuff. Having commandeered the board room for me, she had outfitted it with two telephone extensions and a coffee urn. The exchange operator had been instructed to give priority to all media calls and to pass them through to the office of the Director of Advertising, Ingrid Asboth. Ingrid and her assistants formed a team to sift and assess all calls and shunt them to either Jack or me. Jack would take care of general requests for information, while would-be interviewers were allotted time slots within which they could speak to me on one of my two lines. Because of the demand, Ingrid was already limiting the slots to a maximum of fifteen minutes each.

I don't know how much book business McClelland and Stewart did that day – probably not much; but it was certainly the most hectic day's activity I have ever known.

As I sat down at the board room table, Ingrid gave me a cup of coffee, a stack of marked newspapers, and a list of nine interviews to be completed before noon. A Global Television crew was due at 10:30, which barely gave me time to gulp my coffee and read an account of the incident in the

New York Times. This was a two-column lead whose contents strongly reinforced my decision to fight to the finish if need be.

Author of 'Wolf' Book Barred

"Farley Mowat, a prominent Canadian writer, was denied entry to the United States yesterday under a statute that denies entry to Communists and anarchists.

"The authorities said he was affiliated with leftist organizations and that he could be barred on those grounds . . .

"According to Harry Evans, the editor-in-chief of Atlantic Monthly Press, Mr. Mowat's publisher, the author had been planning to visit the United States to promote his latest book, 'Sea of Slaughter' . . . [which] attacks the human destruction of wildlife in the northeastern seaboard of Canada and the United States.

"Duke Austin, a spokesman for the Immigration Service in Washington, said Mr. Mowat had been listed 'for many, many years' in the service's 'lookout book', a list of people not admissible to the United States for various reasons. Mr. Austin said that Mr. Mowat was on the list under Paragraphs 27 and 28 of Section 212A of the immigration law, which bar anarchists and Communists.

"Mr. Mowat's case was also covered by Immigration Law 235C, the spokesman said, which defines the conditions under which he is barred as 'confidential' . . .

"Mr. Duke said that Mr. Mowat could apply for a hearing and examination to gain entry to the United States, but that granting such a hearing would be the responsibility of the Attorney General. Because the nature of the information against Mr. Mowat is confidential, the spokesman said, the immigration examiner in Toronto was not empowered to lift the ban on his own."

The arrival of the Global Television team put a stop to my reading though not before my temperature had soared. The Global people also had news for me. When the crew was ready to roll, the interviewer asked what I thought of Mr. Ferro's offer to meet me in person to review my file . . . on the Peace Bridge crossing the Niagara River at Buffalo!

I admit that I was tempted. I thought of the photographic opportunities as the wind, howling down the Niagara gorge, blew the mysterious file out of Ferro's frantic hands.

"How come he made that offer to the press, and not me first?" I asked rhetorically, as the camera rolled. "Mr. Ferro knows my name. He knows my phone number. You can tell him, from me, that I'm not going *any*where. I'm the injured party, and he can damn well come to me, preferably with an apology. But tell him, too, that he'll be lucky if we let *him* across *our* border!"

My next interview was by telephone with Betty Kennedy, whose afternoon show on Toronto's largest radio station is a bellwether program. Here is the crux of it.

Intro: Farley Mowat has written 27 books . . . His work has been very widely recognized. He has received the Order of Canada, which is the highest decoration in this country, and he has won the Governor General's Award for his literary work, and he tried yesterday to go to the United States and was turned back at the border and told he could not enter the U.S. He's on the line.

B.K. Farley, why were you going to the United States and what happened?

F.M. Well, I was going to the States to do a ten-day promotion tour for *Sea of Slaughter* . . . I got to the airport and went to the American Immigration . . . and a guy told me, "You are embargoed. You cannot enter the United States." My hair stood straight on end, and I said, "For Christ's sake, why?" and he said, "I am not about to tell you" . . . So I stomped out of the airport, my luggage having gone on to Los Angeles, and . . . since then the whole thing has exploded into a fairly large incident . . .

B.K. Have you ever had any difficulty like this before?

F.M. No, never have. What we first concluded was that it stemmed back to the book I wrote about the Soviet Union – *Sibir* – and the two extensive trips that I took there. On my return from one of those trips, the RCMP phoned me and said they wanted to de-brief me and I was very indignant and said "the hell you will. My briefs are my own, and what's more, I went over to Russia as a private citizen and not as a spy and I'm not going to act as a spy." So that may have been part of it. Then, for the next several years I had a number of contacts with Soviet citizens – almost as many as our hockey team, Team Canada, has had with Russians – my attitude being that Soviet citizens visiting Canada, writers particularly, deserve the same hospitality and friendly greeting that you would give to any foreigners, including Americans. But apparently that's a one-way street – you must be nice to Americans, but you must not be nice to Russians.

B.K.   Where do you go from here? How are you pursuing this, Farley?

F.M.   They have just made an offer – they are getting a little bit jumpy, I think, the American immigration people – that if I will proceed to the Peace Bridge, they will meet me in the centre of the Peace Bridge on neutral territory and review my file – this is the secret file they claim to have on me – and they don't say they will let me in then, but they will review it – and of course, I told them what they could do with that, where they could shove it. There's no bloody way I'd submit to that kind of indignity.

B.K.   You're not curious to know what's in the file?

F.M.   Yes, I'm very curious and we're going to find out, but I'm not going to find out by that route. They're going to come to *me*, or I'd be happy to have them release it to the press.

B.K.   I can't imagine what would be in your file that would be that upsetting to anyone.

F.M.   Well, I'm accused of association with anarchists and Communists. I have certainly associated with Communists because I have met a lot of Soviet citizens and one must assume a lot of them are Communists. I have also had dinner with the last three Soviet Ambassadors to Canada – in fact, I had dinner with the current Soviet Ambassador in Ottawa about eight months ago – in company with the Governor General of Canada.

B.K.   Farley, does it disturb you? Will you make any efforts to clear this up?

F.M.   My point is this – I am innocent until *they* prove *me* guilty. It is not up to me to cringe at their feet and try to prove innocence, nor will I panic at their accusations of communism and crawl under a rock . . . I have told them that if *they* would like to come to Port Hope, to my house if they make an appointment, that I will receive them and I'll listen to what they have to say. I've also told them that I'm not going back to the United States under any circumstances until they send Air Force One to pick me up at Malton, carrying an apology.

B.K.   Thank you, Farley. Good talking with you.

I don't know where the idea of asking for Air Force One – Reagan's enormous Boeing jet – sprang from. Maybe I harbour a secret envy of the flying palaces beloved by modern heads of state, which are the equivalent of the royal yachts of yesteryear. Whatever it was that impelled me, it turned out to be a useful move. The totally outrageous nature of the demand tickled the imagination of the media.

Although I was now leading the attack, Jack was being a most effective chief-of-staff. He initiated a barrage of phone calls to the U.S. Embassy in Ottawa, to our own Department of External Affairs, to both government and opposition parties in Parliament, and to anyone else he thought might help stir up the pot. Nor was Peter Davison remiss. He alerted, in addition to his acquaintances in the press, the American Civil Liberties Union and the prestigious Authors' Guild (part of the Authors' League of America), which fired off a toughly worded statement to the U.S. Attorney General and to Commissioner Alan Nelson, head of the INS. It read, in part:

"Under Supreme Court decisions, the First Amendment [to the Constitution] prevents our government from prohibiting the publication or distribution of Mr. Mowat's book, *Sea of Slaughter*, in the United States . . . [but] the First Amendment is as much affronted by barring Mr. Mowat from speaking in this country as it would be by barring the distribution of his book."

Jack's comment when he heard about this was explosive.

"I bloody well told you, Farley! The Red Menace stuff is camouflage. The anti-eco freaks, the blood-and-guts hunting lobby, *have* to be behind this whole affair. You've really burned their tails!"

Lewis Allen, producer of the film version of *Never Cry Wolf*, had contacted PEN International, a worldwide organization devoted to protecting writers from maltreatment by governments, whether Communist, democratic, or of any other stripe. The president of PEN's American chapter dashed off a telex to George Shultz, U.S. Secretary of State.

"On behalf of the 2,000 writers of American Centre, International PEN, I want to express my surprise and dismay over the denial of a visa to the distinguished Canadian writer, Farley Mowat. It is becoming a real question whether any democracy in Western Europe is as timorous about admitting 'difficult' writers and intellectuals as our McCarran-Walter Act still obliges us to be. These exclusions cost us more international respect than they can ever – assuming they have a practical side – be worth. Yours sincerely. Norman Mailer."

Far from fading, media interest in the story became ever more intense as the day wore on. At 11:10, Canadian Press called for an update . . . at 11:30, a CTV news team videotaped an interview for the network's evening show . . . at 11:55, CBC radio arrived to interview me for the trans-Canada six o'clock news . . . at 12:10, I went live on CBC's *Radio Noon* . . . at 12:15, United Press International was on the phone . . .

On Jack's orders, the "shop" took a break at 12:30, to allow me time to gulp a sandwich and a glass of milk. While I was stuffing my face, my chief-of-staff briefed me on the progress of the battle. He was positively gleeful.

"They're steaming for harbour – God rot their parts! Listen to this Canadian Press release: 'Benedict Ferro, well aware now of Mowat's status in Canada as an articulate and dogged proponent of environmental and literary causes, said his department hoped the matter could be resolved quickly.'

"I'll just bloody well bet they do!" Jack crowed. "But the war ain't won yet. Don't trust the bastards! Hammer 'em, Farley!"

The arrival of a CBC-TV crew for *The National* interrupted this trumpet to arms. However, I hardly needed further goading. The hunted was becoming the hunter, and adrenalin was pouring through my veins like smoking wine. My responses to the CBC-TV interviewer were, as he put it when introducing the segment on the air, "feisty." At the conclusion of the piece, when he asked for my reaction to the Peace Bridge offer to discuss my file, I replied simply, but eloquently, by thumbing my nose toward the south.

The CBC crew was just packing up when Ingrid Asboth slipped into the room and whispered in my ear: "Line two, Farley. It's Joe Clark!"

Her voice was not quite soft enough. The CBC interviewer signalled his cameraman, and the lights flared on again as I picked up the phone.

Now Mr. Clark, as Canadians well know, is a one-time (though short-time) Prime Minister, currently serving his country as Minister of External Affairs – a post equivalent to that of George Shultz as U.S. Secretary of State. I had met Mr. Clark only casually, but he was nevertheless most friendly on the phone, commiserating with me in my predicament and expressing it as his opinion that the whole affair was silly and a mistake.

"Mr. Clark – or may I call you Joe?"

"Please do, Farley."

"I'm afraid I don't think it was originally a mistake, though it may very well have turned out to be one – from the U.S. point of view."

"Yes. Well. Anyway, Farley, you can be sure we are going to do everything we can to clear the matter up . . . My people have already talked to some of theirs and, uh, I think, uh, if you are agreeable to come halfway, they'll come halfway, and it can all, uh, be settled amicably."

"Thank you, Joe. I appreciate that. But I am only prepared to come about one-tenth-of-one-per-cent of the way. I'm the injured party here. So my bottom line is a free trip to Los Angeles in Air Force One, *after* it has delivered President Reagan's letter of apology."

Clark laughed. It may only have been the telephonic effect that made his voice sound a trifle hollow.

"One of my senior people will keep in touch with you," he said in parting. Alas, neither a senior nor a junior ever did.

The TV crew turned off the camera and hustled away, jostling the next arrivals, an interview team from CBC's International Radio, a short-wave service to the world at large. Part of the interview went like this:

Mowat: . . . and pick me up and fly me to Los Angeles, and if they're not prepared to do that, well, screw them.

Announcer: (Laughing) Well, do you think they're going to?

Mowat: I suspect maybe not. But my attitude is basically this: if you are turned down dead trying to enter the United States, and you have no connections to the media, no helmet of power . . . there is nothing you can do. They will not answer questions . . . you are just told to get the hell out, and stay out. And this I find intolerable. *These* are our *friends* across the border?

Announcer: Have you been able to think of . . . that there might be any logical explanation for this?

Mowat: Oh, sure. I know a bunch of Russians, some of them probably Communists. But I've never supported the Communist Party. I have never supported any anarchist or other subversive group. The farthest left I've gone in my life is into the New Democratic Party. And if *that's* subversive, so's the government of Manitoba (which is an NDP government).

Announcer: But what about your writing? Anything about the Soviets, or the war in Vietnam, anything you might have said that was, well, sensitive?

Mowat: Maybe. Maybe. Way back about 1960, I wrote a piece called "Letter To My Son," which suggested to him that unless he and the rest of his generation stood up for Canada, they might one day be welcoming the U.S. Marines to a northern banana republic . . . I also have a predilection for Cuban rum . . . and I did a piece for

the old *Maclean's* magazine called "Greed For
The Yankee Dollar Will Destroy Us All."

Announcer: One U.S. immigration official has said the onus
is now on you to prove yourself eligible to enter
the United States.

Mowat: Isn't that charming? In other words, I'm guilty
until I prove myself innocent! That's not my
concept of democratic justice . . . I have said to
them, *you* prove *me* guilty, baby, and I'll go
along with it . . .

A little while later, Ingrid again hastened into the board
room. This time she took no chances, but passed me a slip of
paper on which she had scribbled:

The Prime Minister is on line one.

With, I admit, a certain amount of trepidation, I picked up
the phone and made myself known.

"Farley? Brian here. I want you to know I think this is the
stupidest thing I've ever heard of. It's an embarrassment to
all concerned."

I agreed that, yes, Sir, it was that all right.

In his wonderfully sonorous and mellifluous way, he went
on to tell me he intended to get in touch with Washington
personally (which conjured up for me a vision of Red
Telephones in the White House). He sympathized with the
position I had taken, but assumed I would accept some com-
promise. When I told him what my minimal terms were, he
chuckled – but briefly and, I thought, less than whole-
heartedly.

Just how embarrassing the situation was for him and the
ruling Conservative Party was graphically illustrated on page
three of the *Toronto Star* the following day. "U.S. 'silly' to
Bar Farley Mowat, Clark Says" was the headline across the
top of the page, and under it was a long account, which included the following:

"Barring Canadian author Farley Mowat from the United
States was 'silly and unwise, and I think that on reflection the
Americans will think it is silly,' says External Affairs Minister
Joe Clark . . . He said he had 'made representations' to

American authorities yesterday . . . Meantime U.S. embassy official Kenneth Bache said there are . . . procedures Mowat could follow if he wanted the decision reversed [but] Mowat said yesterday, 'I told them, as any red-blooded Canadian would, to stuff it.' "

Directly under this story was a large photograph of two smiling ladies. One was Nancy Reagan, the other Mila Mulroney, wife of Canada's Prime Minister. It had been taken, apparently the previous day, in Washington, where Mila was participating in a Nancy-inspired anti-drug crusade. Mila's visit to the Reagans was in the nature of a follow-up to reinforce the mood of the "Shamrock Summit" that had taken place at Quebec City barely a month earlier, featuring as a grand finale Mulroney and Reagan singing on stage before a national TV audience – "When Irish Eyes Are Smiling" – in token of the great affinity between them and their two nations.

"We are more than friends and neighbours and allies," said Reagan at the time. "We are kin . . . [and] there is no more important relationship than our tie with Canada."

It was not difficult to understand why Mr. Mulroney and Mr. Clark found my treatment at the hands of the U.S. government silly, stupid, and embarrassing.

As the afternoon progressed, in turmoil and chaos, the story continued to spread and to gain momentum. American reporters were now making regular telephonic sallies into the Great White North. If I could not be on the West Coast in the flesh, I at least now found myself discovering that region as well as other portions of America through the arcane magic of the electronic age. By four o'clock I had talked to writers and interviewers from the *New York Times*, the *Chicago Tribune*, the *Boston Globe*, RKO radio network, National Public Radio (*All Things Considered*), the *Sacramento Times*, the *Washington Post*, the *Los Angeles Times*, and the Cable News Network.

The CNN interview was live TV, although I could only appear on it as a disembodied voice heard over clips from the film *Never Cry Wolf*. Immediately prior to my "appearance" the program's host had interviewed a spokesman from INS headquarters in Washington. Although hard put to defend or even explain the measures taken against me, this gentleman did go on record as stating, rather plaintively, that: "We also exclude rapists, drug pushers and terrorists – not just Canadians."

It was a comfort to know I was in such varied and interesting company.

During the course of a number of interviews throughout the day, I had made a point of demanding full disclosure by the INS of the contents of their file on me. I wanted it on record that I was happy to dispense with the "confidentiality" the INS spokespeople had insisted they were imposing to protect my privacy.

When the Associated Press phoned from Washington for an update, I volunteered the information that I had been a member of the Fair Play for Cuba Committee (c. 1961); had supported the Campaign for Nuclear Disarmament since its inception.

"Either one might have gotten your name in the lookout book," the Associated Press reporter told me. "And once in, they keep it there 'til death do you part. Which doesn't necessarily mean you are automatically denied entry. What it *does* mean is that if, for some *particular* reason, they want to freeze you out, they can just consult the computer file and pull out whatever suits the need."

"That gives them lots of latitude in my case then," I said. "I'm also a satrap of the Flat Earth Society, by reason of having discovered why a ship sailing away from an observer only *appears* to drop below the horizon."

The AP writer – a woman – could not resist. "So what's the explanation?"

"The earth *is* flat . . . *but corrugated*! Like corrugated cardboard."

"Any other subversive groups you belong to?"

"Well . . . I am an Honorary Herder in the Kolimskaya Reindeer Co-operative in the Yakut Soviet Socialist Republic in Siberia . . ."

"Thank you, Mr. Mowat," she said chuckling. "We'll be keeping in touch."

As it became increasingly apparent that I was not going to accept a "discreet" accommodation that would put a lid on the story, the U.S. authorities did what Jack had warned they might do – they returned to the attack, and with a vengeance.

First news of an escalation of hostilities came from the *Sacramento Bee* in California, one of whose reporters had just been briefed by an INS spokesman who insisted on anonymity. This nameless character gave three reasons for my exclusion. 1. He stated positively that I *was* a member of an outlawed left-wing political group, which, however, he declined to name. 2. Allowing me to enter the U.S.A. would entail a serious espionage risk, he added. 3. Finally, I posed a threat to the armed forces of the United States.

This was indeed heavy artillery and I admit to being a little shaken. Jack was infuriated, but admiring at the same time. "The bastards are making a double-barrelled attempt to quiet the riot. Slug you as hard as they can, but at the same time, offer you a way out of the ring with their damn 'hearings' – one that'll get them off the public hook and move the whole thing behind closed doors."

The *Washington Post* had also heard from INS headquarters, although in this case the accusations against me were posed more subtly. *Post* staff writer George Lardner, Jr., reported that:

"U.S. Immigration spokesman Duke Austin said Mowat had been listed for years in the agency's 'Lookout Book' . . .

"Austin said that the grounds and date for Mowat's listing are 'confidential,' but that they related to at least one of three sections of the McCarran Act.

"One, Section 27, deals with individuals suspected of planning something 'prejudicial to the public interest' or dangerous to 'the welfare, safety or security of the United States.'

"The second, Section 28, is the 'anarchist-communist umbrella.'

"The third, Section 29, involves espionage and sabotage and, specialists say, is generally reserved for actual spies.

" 'We're not going to divulge which ones might apply to Mowat,' Austin said."

This made very scary listening when Lardner read it to me

over the phone (it appeared in the next day's paper); and there was more to come.

As the afternoon neared its end, Malcolm Browne, the staff writer for the *New York Times*, called with this news (the quotation is from the April 25th edition of the *New York Times*):

"A source close to the immigration service, later identified as the U.S. Department of Justice, said the fundamental reason Mowat has been barred was not his politics but statements he was reported to have made threatening violence against the United States armed forces. The source cited an article published March 22, 1968, in the *Ottawa Citizen*, a daily newspaper, quoting Mr. Mowat as having said that he fired a .22 calibre rifle at United States Strategic Air Command aircraft."

Browne asked me if this was true.

For a few moments I was nonplussed, but then, searching my memory, I unearthed what I thought might lie behind the accusation.

It probably harked back, I hazarded, not to 1968, but to 1958 and to the island realm of Newfoundland which, less than a decade earlier, ceased to be a ward of Britain to become Canada's tenth province, and of which I was then in the process of becoming a resident.

In 1940, a year before it entered World War II, the U.S. leased three military bases in Newfoundland from Britain in exchange for some U.S. Navy destroyers of World War I vintage that the allies desperately needed to help contain the Nazi U-boat scourge.

The leases were for ninety-nine years and in 1950, despite Newfoundland's new status as part of Canada, the U.S. insisted on hanging on to them. During the fifties, as the Cold War burgeoned, these bases (together with Goose Bay in Labrador) became major operation centres from which the U.S. Strategic Air Command could threaten the Soviets across the north polar cap. Stephenville and Goose Bay airfields not only hosted B-54 SAC bombers, but also stored hydrogen fusion bombs carried on the so-called "fail-safe" missions. These missions were designed to keep a large proportion of the B-54 bomber force always airborne and *en route* to targets in the U.S.S.R. At a certain point along each aircraft's flight path, the bomber would be recalled by radio. It it should *fail* to receive a recall signal, its crew was under orders to proceed and drop its bombs on the pre-selected Soviet targets.

A great many Canadians, and no few Americans, were horrified at the risks entailed by the fail-safe strategy. Not only was there a real possibility that a nuclear war could be started accidentally if a single bomber failed to respond to its turnback signal, but there were triple dangers to Canadians in having these giant planes flying through our air space. First was the risk that one might crash and detonate its deadly weapons; then there was the possibility that nuclear bombs stored in Newfoundland and Labrador might accidentally explode; finally, there was the absolute certainty that, in the event of war, these arsenals would be attacked by Soviet bombers or nuclear missiles.

To make the situation even more intolerable, the U.S. and Canadian governments *both* denied that SAC bombers carrying nuclear weapons were overflying Canadian territory, or that such weapons were stored on Canadian soil. These denials could hardly have been intended to fool the Soviets, who almost certainly knew the truth – they were deliberately designed to fool the Canadians into becoming nuclear accomplices of America.

How did I know about the bombs? A number of U.S. servicemen stationed in Newfoundland (some married to Newfoundland women), together with civilian employees on the various bases, were, not surprisingly, disturbed about the presence of these weapons, which some claimed to have seen with their own eyes. They communicated their distress to my friend, Harold Horwood, then associate editor of the *St. John's Evening Telegram* in the island's capital. One irate informant even volunteered to lead us to the location of a nuclear weapons storage depot near Stephenville which, for good and obvious reasons, was not on the leased base itself but some distance away in the wooded defiles of the Blomidon Mountains.

One foggy evening in September, 1958, over the second (it may have been the third) bottle of rum, Horwood and I and a few like-minded romantics decided the time had come to do something about this situation. We then and there constituted ourselves the Newfoundland Revolutionary Society, dedicated, first, to ridding the island of foreign military forces, and then to freeing the world from the looming threat of nuclear dissolution. By the time dawn broke clammy and chill over St. John's harbour, we had a plan of action.

We would drive across the island to Stephenville (and to say it was to consider it done) carrying a gallon or two of that singularly ferocious Newfoundland rum called Screech. We would approach the secret SAC bomb arsenal in a carefree way and offer to share our grog with what our informant assured us would be a bored and merely token guard detachment. When the Screech had done its stuff, we would tenderly remove one of the smaller bombs, transport it to Red Indian Lake in the interior, and drop it gingerly into the almost bottomless depths of that great body of water. We would then announce that *we had The Bomb*, invite all foreign military forces to depart the island – then do a *Mouse That Roared.**

If the U.S. armed forces dared pursue us, by either land or air, we would stand them off with swiling guns – smooth bore muzzleloaders with which outport Newfoundlanders have hunted seals ("swiles" in local argot) for centuries.

The external fog was thinning when we issued our manifesto – which we phrased as if it were a *fait accompli* – and rolled off to bed.

I'm afraid it had no great impact at the time, although after I mentioned the presence of atomic bombs at Stephenville base during a TV appearance that autumn, the Canadian Prime Minister of the day, John Diefenbaker, replied that not a speck, no, not a whiff of any atomic weapon existed or ever would on Canada's sacred soil while his government stood guard in Ottawa. He later indicated in the House of Commons that he felt Farley Mowat had somewhat exagger-

---

* *The Mouse That Roared* is a satirical book by Leonard Wibberley, later made into a comedy film starring Peter Sellers, in which a small country forced disarmament on the major powers by confiscating, then threatening to detonate, a nuclear bomb.

ated the situation. Diefenbaker was not wholly without a sense of humour.

I told the essence of this story to Browne, who asked if he could print it. I had, of course, not told it simply to amuse him. Now that the U.S. authorities were zeroing in on me with their heaviest guns, I was ready to retaliate with the most powerful weapons at *my* disposal. Browne's straight-faced version of this tale, which was repeated by most major U.S. media, set the tone for much of what would follow.

By 5:30 p.m., Jack and I and the loyal McClelland and Stewart staff were exhausted. I had decided it was time to make a break for home, and someone had phoned David Brooks to come and get me. As I was leaving the building, Ingrid gave me a sheaf of telegrams, telexes, and telephone messages to read in the car. Some were from Canadians, commiserating with me in my difficulty; however, to my considerable surprise, the great majority were from Americans apologizing for what their government had done to me – and urging me on to battle. A telegram from a Washington writer was typical. "*Nil Carborundum Illigitimo*" – atrocious Latin for "Don't let the bastards grind you down." These messages provided a heartening culmination to a hectic day in the trenches.

However, it was not quite ended yet. At home again, I had a long drink in company with my much-relieved wife while I briefed her on what had been happening. I had almost forgotten that I was supposed to be in California when the phone rang. The caller was Michael Robertson, a staff writer with the *San Francisco Chronicle*. Having assured me that my absence in California had not gone unnoticed, he told me the outline for a lead story that would appear the following morning.

"Canadian writer-naturalist Farley Mowat won't be on the Coast this week, sipping bitter coffee in local bookstores, signing autographs and shaking uncalloused hands and spreading the message contained in *Sea of Slaughter*, his latest book – if we're determined to destroy ourselves let's not take the rest of the world with us.

"Mowat's exclusion has caused an international miniscandal, so painful to Canadian sensibilities that he received a personal promise from Prime Minister Mulroney that the PM would immediately contact Washington and get it all straightened out.

"Mowat hasn't heard from Mulroney since. From his home in Port Hope, he hooted with laughter: 'It is very rarely that a Canadian Prime Minister accomplishes anything in Washington. After all, we Canadians are hardly more than house slaves to the American Empire. Of course, we are better off than the field slaves of South America.'

"Mowat says he was delighted he was kept off the plane. 'This is the best thing that could have happened for Canada, and maybe for the United States. The arbitrary and unjustified exclusion of Canadians – and others – is a long-time U.S. practice, but there is no recourse for the ordinary person. They can't even find out what the charges are. They have to crawl on their bellies to the I.N.S. . . . but fortunately I'm in a position to make an outcry about it.'

"Mowat does not think he will be getting to San Francisco soon – however, 'If you see Air Force One overhead, that will be me.'

"Meantime what can the average person do to protect the endangered species? *Sea of Slaughter* was written to raise that question.

" 'Look around at what little remains of natural life,' Mowat says, 'and then stand ready to break your heart and your ass if needs be to try to save what's left.' "

III

Thursday, April 25

The schedule for the rest of your stay in Los Angeles is not yet fully confirmed. Several radio and television shows are upcoming. You will be taken on a book store tour, autographings to be arranged. Publicity visits to Hollywood and the Walt Disney Studios are in the works . . .

I rose very early Thursday morning, loaded our two black dogs – Tom and Lily – into the car, and drove across the railway tracks to the shore of Lake Ontario for a walk on the beaches. Flotillas of Canada geese floated not far offshore, loudly discussing the next lap of their journey north. In my mind's eye, I saw myself voyaging with them, all thoughts of visiting America temporarily banished.

The dogs and I were alone on the beach, but as we returned to the car a Canadian National Railway foreman hailed me. "Hey . . . Farley! Hear you got turned back at the Mexican border, eh? Smuggling rum? Or porn?"

I did not try to put him straight, but muttered to myself in Spanish and drove home. As I entered the house the phone was ringing. It was 7:25 a.m.

On Wednesday, the story of my exclusion had belonged largely to Canada, but by Thursday morning the centre of gravity had shifted south of the border, and any hopes Claire and I might have entertained that things would quiet down soon dissipated. Before we took the phone off the hook near midnight, we had received well over seventy-five calls (we lost count with the seventy-fifth), and I had given more than thirty interviews, the majority of them to American press, radio, television, and magazines.

Canadians had not, however, lost interest, and editorial comments were beginning to appear. From the East Coast, the *Cape Breton Post* printed this one.

Snubbing Farley

"Farley Mowat, one of Canada's most popular authors, is the latest to receive a dose of good old American hospitality . . . he was refused entry to the States because he is suspected of being a Communist, anarchist or subversive.

"That's nonsense! Mr. Mowat is no danger to democracy either in Canada or the United States. He is a respected writer who has even won several American literary awards . . .

"In a diplomatic understatement, External Affairs Minister Joe Clark agreed that the U.S. action 'was not wise' . . . Mr. Mowat's American publisher believes the barring of the author is just a 'low-level [bureaucratic] blunder'. However both he and Mr. Clark are probably underestimating the matter. This is not the first time U.S. authorities have banned foreign writers from their country, which Americans like to think of as a bastion of freedom and tolerance.

"Last year, U.S. immigration refused to allow several Italian and Latin-American authors into the country to attend a conference. This was not some bureaucratic blunder, but a firm standing order.*

"One is also reminded of the attempt to ban the Canadian nuclear disarmament movie made by the National Film Board, *If You Love This Planet*. Later, this same film won an Oscar.

"Banning Farley Mowat is an affront and an insult to Canada as well as to the man himself. An apology is in order from the United States government."

Far away, in western Canada, the *Medicine Hat News* editorialized:

"Farley Mowat is fuming over a bureaucrat's decision to

---

* This was a conference on Free Trade in Ideas sponsored by the American Civil Liberties Union. Guests who were prevented from entering the U.S.A. included Hortensia Allende, widow of Salvadore Allende, the last democratically elected president of Chile; Dario Fo, award-winning Italian actor and playwright, one of whose performances was about to open in New York; Franca Rame, Italian actress and co-performer with Fo; Gabriel Garcia Marquez, 1982 Nobel Prize winner in Literature; General Nino Pasti, former Deputy Supreme Commander, Allied Forces in Europe; Denis Brutus, South African poet; and others.

deny him entry into the United States but he should really be thanking the little nobody.

"Mr. Mowat was to visit the United States to promote his latest book, but was informed he could not enter because of his Communist connections.

"Farley, a Red? . . .

"Wholly innocent.

"But try telling that to a file clerk weaned on a diet of 'Better dead than Red' and 'Russia is an evil empire'."

The morning edition of Canada's national newspaper, the *Globe and Mail*, was delivered to my door by a grinning, middle-aged carrier, an old friend, who now told me he had always suspected me of subversion because I voted for the New Democratic Party and drank vodka. The paper contained this editorial.

"It took hours of intensive research to narrow it down, but it is worth going to some trouble to find out why the United States would not let Canadian author Farley Mowat into the country . . . His dossier [includes] his provocative writings about the growing sterility of freshwater lakes in North America, passionate outcries about the destruction of life on earth, and the fact – doubtless coughed up by a hysterical computer – that he has visited the Soviet Union.

"Surely it couldn't be that visit alone that persuaded the U.S. authorities to pounce on this kilted subversive? Or do we finally come to the reason for President Ronald Reagan's reluctance to visit the Soviet Union: that he might not be allowed to come back home?"

Bruce Levett, in a syndicated column for the Canadian Press, had fun with the issue.

" 'Farley Mowat?' she gasped.

" 'So it would seem.'

" 'OUR Farley? He who writes about wolves and whales and sail boats that decline to float?'

" 'I know of no other such.'

" 'A case of mistaken identity, do you think?' she whispered.

" 'Hardly. How could anyone possibly mistake Farley Mowat for anyone else?' . . .

" 'Could it be the beard, possibly? It does tend to get a bit straggly between weedings,' she offered.

" 'Probably not. Can it be that the eyes are just a touch too close together?'

"She snorted.

" 'I like his eyes. However, I am not all that enthused concerning his kilt.'

"He shook his head.

" 'No, it can't be that. I doubt that even the Americans would exclude someone just because they disapproved of the tilt of his kilt.' . . .

" 'Attempting to keep the world safe for democracy may, indeed, be admirable – but keeping it safe from Farley Mowat?'

" 'Have they nothing better to do?' she snarled."

Expressions of Canadian concern extended beyond our borders as Toronto columnist, Beverley Slopen, wrote in the U.S. magazine, *Publishers' Weekly*: "The INS could hardly have singled out a more famous and well-connected Canadian. Mowat, whose books have been translated into more than 40 languages, is a close friend of Edward Schreyer, former Governor-General of Canada, who stepped down last year . . . Mowat and his wife Claire accompanied the Schreyers in 1983 on a state visit to five Nordic countries, Farley as companion to the Governor-General and Claire as lady-in-waiting to Mrs. Schreyer. They also were frequent guests of the Schreyers at Government House, all situations that presumably involved security clearance."

The support of fellow citizens was comforting. If, as the *Toronto Sun* quoted me as saying (and I said it), "Joe McCarthy is rising from his grave," at least his ghost was making small headway convincing my countrymen that I was a sinister threat to the Western world.

However, I was still uncertain what the overall American media reaction would be, and apprehensive that it might follow where the INS was trying to lead.

I need not have been concerned. By noon, it was evident that my refusal to take the INS seriously, or to allow it to take *me* seriously, was swinging the tide in my favour. Typical of U.S. coverage was an Associated Press dispatch by Dolores

Barclay, datelined New York, from which the following excerpts come.

"Canadian nature writer Farley Mowat's world is one in which snow geese whiten the sky . . . However, a quagmire of controversy also fills the landscape for the author of 'Never Cry Wolf' . . .

"In a telephone interview Thursday from his home in Port Hope, Ontario, Mowat said he wasn't given a reason for not being allowed to fly to Los Angeles . . .

"Kathleen Lang, a press officer for the State Department, said Wednesday that Mowat belonged to a 'proscribed organization' but refused to say what it was. Mowat says he is a member of the New Democratic Party, a left-leaning minority political party in Canada.* . . .

"Mowat plans another book soon, one he says will give him pleasure to write.

" 'I want to write about the funny, amusing events of my life,' he said. 'It will probably end with this little contretemps with the INS, but I have to wait and see how this all ends.' "

The *San Francisco Chronicle* quoted me, with sweet reasonableness, as "considering moderating his demands. 'I might accept a letter from the vice-president and a two-engine executive aircraft. They are actually more fun to fly.' "

Another and more sombre story appeared in the *Boston Globe*, which included a quote from Peter: "Peter Davison, senior editor of the Atlantic Monthly Press, said: 'It seems tragic that Farley, whose books have been published in scores of languages and who has travelled around the globe in search of a deeper understanding of mankind's relationship to nature, should be denied access to the U.S., of all places.' "

And then there was Chico, which was not taking the loss of Mowat lightly. Anguished telegrams from Michael Bauman and other staff members at the university had made that clear. The Chico *Enterprise-Record* was giving the story extensive coverage. Staff writer Kevin Flanagan reported:

---

* The NDP is the third largest federal party and polled 22 per cent of the vote in the last federal election. As noted earlier, it currently forms the government of the province of Manitoba, and of Yukon Territory.

"Chico State University President Robin Wilson characterized as 'absurd' the barring of renowned Canadian writer Farley Mowat and compared the immigration service's action to the red-baiting of many years ago . . .

" 'Having been a professional Commie-fighter for several years in the CIA, I find this completely absurd,' said Wilson, a former intelligence employee. 'To bar a Canadian who may have some vague radical background evokes the Red-baiting, witch-hunts and the domestic security monster that has haunted U.S. politics since the days of J. Edgar Hoover,' he added. 'I doubt if Mr. Mowat would come to the United States now under any circumstances.'

"Michael Bauman said reaction ranged from outrage to shame. 'I'm amazed at the response. I didn't realize how popular he was.' "

I hadn't realized it myself, but Chico was clearly some special place. Where else would I have been likely to find an ex-CIA agent coming to my defence?

Just after lunch (consisting of soup drunk out of a cup because the telephone left me no time for anything better), a Washington reporter called to tell me that the incident of the SAC bombers was more complex than I had realized.

"The people at State tell me they've never heard of your plot to steal one of our atomic bombs. They seem pretty upset by the failure of our intelligence services to get onto it. So we called the *Ottawa Citizen* and got them to dig out the story State is using.

"It says that in March of 1968, you turned down the command of something called the Col. J. Sutherland Brown Volunteer Brigade whose purpose, and I quote, was to defend Canada against an invasion by U.S. Strategic Air Force bombers carrying out simulated attacks at the 500-foot level every fifteen minutes over the Saskatchewan prairies, with Canadian government sanction.

"You are quoted as saying you turned down the command because, although you had fired your .22 at SAC bombers flying hydrogen bombs over your backyard in Newfoundland, you wouldn't take command because the Volunteers were only going to use blanks. It ends with this quote from you:

'After all, we fought the Yanks in 1812 and kicked them the hell out – but not with blanks.'

"Would you care to comment, Mr. Mowat?"

It all came pouring back to me. "Sure," I said. "I'd be delighted. You got a couple of minutes?"

Col. J. Sutherland Brown was Canada's chief-of-staff during the latter part of the 1920s. A life-long student of Canadian-American history, he had concluded that the United States was some day going to try to make good on an oft-repeated boast (or threat, as Canadians saw it) to take Canada under its wing.

Brown was an expert on American attempts to absorb Canada, including the War of 1812 and the U.S.-backed Fenian raids of the 1860s (which bear an uncanny resemblance to the U.S.-backed "contras" raiding present-day Nicaragua). He knew all about James Knox Polk who, in 1845, became the eleventh president of the United States and devoted most of his term to expanding his nation's territories – at the expense of Mexico, which lost California and much of what is now the American Southwest; and of the future Canada, which was deprived of the Oregon Territory, then under British ownership. Polk also supported the Democratic Party of his day in its ambition to seize most of what would eventually become the habitable parts of the Dominion of Canada, under the jingoist slogan "55° 40 ′ or Fight!" Sutherland Brown was also fully cognizant of the widespread American belief in Manifest Destiny, which went so far as to envisage Canada's inclusion in a greater co-prosperity hemisphere, under the Stars and Stripes.

So convinced was Sutherland Brown that Canada's future was at risk that he directed the Canadian military staff in the late 1920s to prepare an operation plan for repulsing an American invasion. This plan was maintained with great secrecy – Prime Minister Mackenzie King, warm admirer of the U.S.A. and no strong opponent of the idea of Manifest Destiny, seems never to have been told about it – until the outbreak of World War II posed a more urgent threat, and Sutherland Brown's preparations to defend his country were consigned to the archives.

However, in the 1960s there was still a considerable weight

of opinion in Canada mirroring the late Colonel's uneasiness about American intentions. I shared the feeling. In fact, I had founded the Canadian Committees for Independence, a short-lived organization dedicated to defending and strengthening Canada's sovereignty in economic and political fields. Another group, but one with a single specific purpose, was also formed during those days. This was the Col. J. Sutherland Brown Volunteer Brigade. Its *raison d'être* was to make such a nuisance of itself that giant SAC bombers, which had been granted permission by a subservient Canadian administration to practise low-level runs over the province of Saskatchewan (something no state of the union would permit), would be forced to cease and desist.

The Brigade's organizers consulted me about ways and means. I suggested they acquire a quantity of the large red balloons used by weather recording stations, hide them in convenient gullies and coulees along the flight paths followed by the bombers, and release them at the appropriate moments. I estimated that the sudden appearance of these great crimson globes wafting upward in front of them would make even the most case-hardened bomber pilots claw for altitude. It followed with iron logic that, if they could not fly low without having the wits scared out of them, they would buzz off home and leave Saskatchewan to the wheat farmers, gophers, and grasshoppers.

Although my plan was accepted, I declined command of the Brigade, *not* because the Volunteers refused to use live ammo but simply because I was otherwise engaged. The report in the *Ottawa Citizen* was full of – hyperbole.

All this I told the reporter, who seemed a trifle dazed.

"You kidding me?" he asked faintly.

I assured him I was not.

"Well, did you ever actually *fire* your .22 at SAC bombers flying over your house in Newfoundland?"

"Of course not," I answered shortly. "Do you think I'm mad? Why, suppose I'd brought one down! The consequent explosion would have eliminated half of Newfoundland."

"How high were they anyhow?"

"Couldn't say for sure, but about five miles, I'd guess. You could only spot them with binoculars."

"Yes," he said thoughtfully. "Well, thank you, Mr. Mowat. Now you take care, you hear?"

He was a charming chap, but then, so were most of the American reporters with whom I came in contact.

The Associated Press was quick to catch the updated version of the bomber story, and late that evening put it on the wire.

"Mowat said his 1968 remarks about U.S. planes were made in 'jest' and reflected his annoyance that U.S. aircraft, which he believes were carrying hydrogen bombs, were passing through Canadian airspace.

" 'I got a little annoyed about this,' he said, 'and stated publicly that if they didn't stop intruding into my personal airspace, I'd blast them out of the skies with my trusty little .22. Of course I never actually shot at them because if I'd hit one and it had fallen on me, I'd have been vaporised.' "

The INS seems to have been disappointed by the press's reception to its "threat to the U.S. armed forces" blockbuster, and its officials now began to back away from this excuse for banning me. The *Globe and Mail* reported:

"The stalemate continues between Farley Mowat and U.S. immigration officials who won't let him into the United States until he proves he isn't a Communist, anarchist or subversive . . . U.S. officials still won't reveal what evidence they have against him but the *New York Times* and the *Washington Post* have reported Mr. Mowat was barred because an *Ottawa Citizen* article of March 22, 1968 quoted Mr. Mowat as saying he had fired a rifle at U.S. military aircraft carrying atomic bombs.

" 'We certainly wouldn't condone that kind of activity,' Duke Austin, spokesman for the I.N.S., said in an interview, 'but I don't think this incident, in itself, would be enough to get Mr. Mowat on the list . . . we don't even know if he really did shoot at the plane.' "

After making the obvious point that my threat to wing SAC bombers was "only spoofing," George Lardner, Jr., of the *Washington Post* announced the arrival of reinforcements to my side.

"Representative Barney Frank (D., Mass.) said that he will

introduce legislation to repeal long-standing provisions of U.S. immigration law allowing foreigners to be denied entry solely because of their political beliefs and affiliations.

"Frank, a member of the House immigration sub-committee, said, 'We have to stop acting as if admission to the United States is an enormous favour we are doing for foreigners.' He said travel policies should be regarded 'as a matter of freedom of association for our own citizens.'

"Frank's statement was sparked by U.S. refusal to allow a prominent Canadian writer to enter the United States . . . and by continuing delays in allowing the entry of a Nicaraguan cabinet minister.

"Nicaragua's Minister of Culture, Ernesto Cardenal, was forced to delay a 10-day U.S. speaking tour while State Department officials considered his week-old visa application.

"The Canadian writer, Farley Mowat, . . . said he will do everything he can 'to bring pressure to change the system' that kept him from flying to Los Angeles to promote his newest book . . .

"Mowat denied that he was a member of any subversive organization . . . I.N.S. District Director Ben Ferro said that 'we haven't refused Mowat admission' yet and would not do so unless he first meets with I.N.S. officials, something Mowat refuses to do. Ferro said, however, that Mowat could get a waiver but only 'if we find him to be inadmissible. In our judgment, we haven't completed the inspection so we haven't refused him admission.' "

The INS hadn't refused me admission? I found my head swimming as I tried to make sense out of this murky example of bureaucratic gobbledegook.

Meanwhile, on the West Coast of America, the press was becoming increasingly partisan, as witness this editorial in the *San Francisco Chronicle*.

A Clumsy Act

"By barring Canadian author Farley Mowat the I.N.S. has taken one of those clumsy, left-footed lurches that seem all too characteristic of the agency. The reasons for barring

Mowat are locked somewhere deep in the files on laws against visits by Communists, anarchists and other nasty types, so we cannot grapple directly with the cause.

"But it seems unlikely that this Canadian author and naturalist presents any kind of real threat to his neighbours south of the border. He's the man who has written so evocatively about endangered wildlife – whales, seals, and wolves – that inhabit our lands and seas. He's a prickly, talented person; one fully endowed with the sense of humour that our immigration types so noticeably lack . . .

"If the whole affair weren't such an unfortunate example of insensitive bureaucracy in action, it might make a hilarious movie."

As criticism of it mounted within the U.S.A., the INS began sidestepping or, as they say in the vernacular, trying to cover its ass. In doing so, it exposed an exceedingly sensitive portion of Canada's anatomy. The story was broken by the Washington bureau of the Canadian Press.

"Canadian author Farley Mowat was denied entry to the United States this week because of information provided to U.S. authorities by the Royal Canadian Mounted Police, a U.S. government official said.

"The official, who sought anonymity, refused to disclose the nature of the information but said it was provided in 1968.*

"Duke Austin, a spokesman for the I.N.S., had confirmed earlier that Mowat's name was contained in what is known as the 'look-out book' . . . The Canadian names in that book are 'based on information provided by the R.C.M.P., no question about that,' Austin said in an interview . . . 'The two governments have traditionally shared intelligence informa-

---

* I realized when I saw this account that I had made a tactless error in recommending *red* balloons to the Col. J. Sutherland Brown Volunteers, even though they were never used. The Volunteers were unable to obtain the necessary helium gas, whose export by the only major helium producer, the United States, had been embargoed under the Strategic Resources Act. Helium had been selected because it is non-explosive, whereas the alternative – hydrogen – might conceivably have endangered the bombers.

tion on individuals.' Austin would not say for certain whether the R.C.M.P. provided information on Mowat in particular, 'But I'd say that would be one helluva good guess.' . . .

"In Canada, the previous Liberal government operated on the understanding the I.N.S. was respecting a 1980 agreement to purge its files of security information obtained from the R.C.M.P. . . .

"The deputy associate commissioner of the I.N.S. sent a letter to New Democrat MP Svend Robinson in November 1983 acknowledging formal termination of the information exchange agreement in May 1980.

[But] "A review of our files failed to provide any information pertaining to an agreement to purge information provided by the Royal Canadian Mounted Police."

Here was a pretty kettle of fish, and the fat was in the fire in Ottawa, if I may be permitted a mix of culinary metaphors. Public disclosure that Canada's famed Red Coats had for long been keeping tabs on their fellow citizens for the benefit of a paranoid U.S. immigration service was a severe embarrassment to Canadian lawgivers. Even worse was the revelation that Canada's belated attempt to wipe the record clean had not met with the approval of U.S. authorities.

One of the first reporters to call me about this new development was a Soviet correspondent based in Ottawa.

"How you feel," he said solemnly, "about discovery secret police spy on you for Americans?"

"No worry," I replied breezily. "It's been going on for years. We're used to it."

"Not being angry?" he asked, obviously disappointed.

"Not a bit . . . wait a moment; there's some interference on the line . . . constable? You there, constable! Do something about your tape recorder! I can't hear my party. Thank you . . . now, where were we? Far from being annoyed, I'm actually quite pleased to know the Mounties are keeping up to the mark. Always willing to do a favour for fellow spooks. All in the family sort of thing, if you know what I mean."

"Da . . . I think . . . very confusing. Thank you, Mr. Mowat."

I was not entirely having the poor fellow on. Most informed Canadians knew about these surreptitious activities of the RCMP. As a responsible citizen, I had even made it my practice to be co-operative. During the late 1950s and through most of the 1960s, I voluntarily dispatched confidential reports to the RCMP Commissioner detailing those of my activities which I thought might excite his interest.

Examples include a detailed account of a masked ball that Claire and I attended during an Atlantic crossing on the MV *Alexander Pushkin* and a play-by-play description of how, while visiting me, the Siberian writer Yuri Rytkheu was seduced by a singularly hairy lady who, I concluded, must have been one of the Commissioner's operatives.

My finest confidential report was probably an account of a 1968 penetration of the U.S.S.R. Embassy in Ottawa conducted by me, my wife, and my father, Angus.

Actually, we went to the Embassy by invitation of the Ambassador, Ivan Schpedko, an avid fisherman who, having caught a number of brook trout, had asked us to come and enjoy a meal, which he promised to cook himself.

He was as good as his word, and also a good cook; and the meal the four of us shared with the First Secretary of the Embassy was a jovial affair, well lubricated with vodka and Armenian cognac.

As midnight approached, we Canadians concocted a plan to subvert the loyalties of these unsuspecting Russians. My father and I had both come to dinner kilted, and we now persuaded our hosts that they should allow themselves to be inducted into the mysteries of a Scottish clan. We then inveigled them into exchanging their formal black trousers for our kilts. Since both Russians were tall and heavyset, and Angus and I were small and lean, the mutal fit left something to be desired. We capped it – literally – by putting our Scots bonnets on their heads.

Angus then proposed that we adjourn to the flat, second-storey roof of the Embassy. This overlooked a row of private houses on adjacent Charlotte Street, one of which had borne a "For Rent" sign for many years. It was general knowledge, however, that it was occupied by sleuths of the RCMP security service, presumably equipped with the latest in espionage gadgets such as infrared cameras and directional microphones.

Part of the induction ceremony, Angus explained, was to symbolically recreate Bonnie Prince Charlie's approach to the Battle of Culloden. To this end, he lined us up and set us marching around the roof to the stirring music of a pibroch, which he played, without benefit of pipes, by holding his nose with one hand while beating on his Adam's apple with the other and at the same time emitting a high-pitched squeal. This made an arresting skirl and we assumed the spooks across the street would be alerted by it.

The third time round I took my cue from Angus and, as we passed the Charlotte Street side, shouted an order in my best Company Commander style.

"GENERAL SALUTE . . . EYEEEEEES RIGHT!"

My intention was to bring the two Russians full-face to the unseen cameras so that their Scottish deviation would be forever preserved on file. Unfortunately, our hosts chose to add a fillip of their own. They saluted the Watchers In The Night with thumbs to noses and fingers madly waggling.

In my report to the Commissioner, I begged his forgiveness for this act of *lèse-majesté*, but do not know if he ever granted it since he never favoured me even with an acknowledgment. Perhaps he was afraid he might blow my cover.

Ah, the escapades of youth – or even middle age.

Although it has not previously occurred to me, I now began to wonder if, in addition to clippings from newspapers, the Mounties had also forwarded my reports on myself to the U.S. authorities. Perhaps *these* comprised the secret information that the INS officials refused to disclose. If so, I could appreciate their dilemma. One could imagine what the *Washington Post*, for example, would have done with the Schpedko "incident."

The day was now drawing to an end, for which Claire and I were immeasurably grateful. I was also grateful for the return of my errant suitcase, which was delivered by a polite Canadian customs official. He explained that, normally, owners of such wandering luggage had to collect it themselves at the airport. However, in view of what had recently happened in the U.S. Customs and Immigration department at Pearson, his boss had decided to make an exception in my case.

At this juncture Ingrid Asboth phoned in some excitement to tell me that the NBC *Today Show* wanted to do a live interview with me first thing Friday morning. She explained that it would be a "remote" from a Toronto studio. Since this would entail being on the road at dawn, I was less than enthusiastic. However, I allowed myself to be persuaded on the assurance that it would be of service to the cause.

There were two final telegrams. The first was from the Canadian High Commissioner's residence in Canberra.

COME BACK TO AUSTRALIA STOP WE WILL LET YOU IN
Ed and Lily Schreyer.

The second was from a lady in Tennessee.

HOW COULD THE AUTHOR AND OWNER OF THE BOAT WHO WOULDN'T FLOAT NOT REPEAT NOT BE A SUBMERSIVE STOP THE INS IS NEVER WRONG.

On which note, we went contentedly, if wearily, to bed.

Reproduced courtesy Alan King.

IV
Friday, April 26

*Prime Time Limo will call for you at your hotel at 7:15
a.m. to take you to Los Angeles Airport.*
Depart Los Angeles 8:52 a.m., Western Flight #103.
Arrive Sacramento 10:25 a.m.
*Michael Bauman from Chico University will pick you up
and take you to Chico. He will be your host for the weekend.*
*A showing of "Never Cry Wolf" at the university at 7:00
p.m. will be followed by your address, a question period and
informal entertainment.*

Instead of taking my departure from the Beverly Wilshire in
my Prime Time Limo, 7:15 a.m. found me crammed into a
hot, foul-smelling, and airless cubicle in the basement of a
Toronto television station. Strange noises intermingling with
snatches of unidentifiable music whiffled and mumbled in my
single earphone, which kept slipping out of my ear. The microphone, pinned to my shirt, was equally intractable, with a
tendency to drop out of its clip and into' my lap. A cup of
ersatz coffee stood cold and bitter on the worn table behind
which I perched on a hard stool. Sharing this cramped
simulacrum of a spy-movie interrogation room with me was a
cameraman; but he was hidden behind a battery of blinding
lights. I was not at ease.

A disembodied voice suddenly whispered in my ear: *"Today Show . . .* Mr. Mowat?"

"Here, Sir," I muttered, in a conditioned reflex. But my
microphone had fallen out again. I fumbled it back in place
and shouted wildly: *"Yes! I'm here! I'M HERE!"*

"Don't *do* that, Mr. Mowat . . . stand by . . . thirty
seconds."

So began my interview with hostess Jane Pauley, whose

name nobody had told me and whom I could not see because there was no TV monitor in my crypt. Nor could I see the other guest, but at least I knew who he was. Benedict Ferro.

With slimy hands, I pawed the notes I had made in preparation for this moment, scanning them desperately for the most effective opening line: offer him a hundred grand against his INS job if he can show any evidence I am a Commie, ever was, or ever wanted to be? . . . Tell him he doesn't look like a reborn Joe McCarthy but he sure as hell acts like one? . . . If I'm a threat to the United States armed forces, then God help America? . . . Is it true that some of your own citizens call the INS the Inquisition and Nazification Service? . . .

"Good morning, Mr. Mowat, and welcome to the *Today Show*."

I don't have a clear recollection of what transpired thereafter. I do know the whole thing was over in two or three minutes, and that I lost my earphone at least once. I also recall that, after some preliminary fencing, our hostess asked Mr. Ferro the essential reason for my exclusion, and that he proffered the incident of my .22 and the SAC bombers.

"We certainly do take more seriously perhaps than Mr. Mowat the firing at a United States aircraft – or even the *symbolic* firing at a United States aircraft."

When the hostess asked me if I had truly done such a dastardly thing as shoot at an American bomber, I replied: "I'd be scared to do that. It might fall on my house."

I went on to explain that I was a victim of "Canada's good neighbour policy" as a result of which the RCMP had supplied the INS with a dossier on me. I concluded by suggesting that perhaps the INS might function more humanely if it cultivated a better sense of humour.

Then it was over. And, as so often happens, all of my best lines had been left unsaid. I arrived back in Port Hope in a somewhat deflated mood, in time to intercept the mailman as he approached my door. He was carrying an enormous bundle, which he thrust into my arms.

"You keep this up," he said, smiling, "and I'm going to have to ask for extra pay. You think you'll really get Reagan's plane?"

In my current mood I was not optimistic about that, but it would not have done to admit as much.

"Sure," I replied. "As soon as the President gets home from visiting German cemeteries, it'll be on its way."

To my relief, the telephone remained relatively quiet for the rest of the morning, producing only two requests for interviews – one from radio station KOA in Denver, and one from WPLP in Tampa, Florida. However, the media were still very much on the story, as a news release from the Council of Canadians demonstrated.

" 'The refusal of the American government to admit . . . Farley Mowat, is a warning to Canadians and Americans alike', said Prof. John Trent, National Policy Chairperson, in Ottawa today.

"Stopping Mowat at the border is an indication that behind the big smile resides a closed and narrow mind . . . Of course, the U.S. Immigration officials have refused to say why they have blocked Mowat's entrance. One possibility . . . is his role as a conservationist. We know the Reagan administration's record on destroying environmental agencies . . . and refusing to negotiate on acid rain with Canada, or on the Law of the Sea Treaty. We also saw the heavy-handed action of the U.S. Justice Department which labelled the Canadian film, *If You Love This Planet*, as propaganda.

"The lesson for all of us is that . . . the American authorities no longer seem to be able to discriminate between foreigners who may be a real threat to the state and those critics who may have a different opinion from the current administration . . .

"We know there are many millions of Americans who will agree with our denunciation of this narrow-minded act in stopping a widely respected Canadian author at the border. We call upon our American friends to put pressure on their government . . ."

Professor Trent was not crying in the wilderness. The already positive reaction from the United States was becoming ever more supportive.

"A Writer Wrongly Barred" was the heading of an editorial in the *San Francisco Examiner*:

"A note to the U.S. Immigration and Naturalization Service: Kindly stop protecting us from writers whose ideas or background you dislike. It is embarrassing to the United States when you prevent writers from entering this country, and an insult to the intelligence of the citizens you serve.

"The INS may have been acting within the law when it barred Canadian writer Farley Mowat, but the agency plainly doesn't understand that a more important principle applies: in this nation, the free exchange of ideas is encouraged. This is a simple, civic-book maxim, but one that apparently escaped the bureaucrats responsible for this ludicrous decision.

"Mowat . . . was set to tour the United States to promote his latest book . . . [which] criticizes the fishing industry and laments the destruction of North American coastal wildlife. However, readers who would like to discuss these ideas with the author won't be able to, for some INS whiz discovered that Mowat's name is listed in the agency's 'lookout book' . . .

"The upshot of the foolish INS action is that U.S. readers have access to Mowat's books, but not to the writer himself. Is there a point in this absurdity? Whatever his political views, Mowat does not seem much of a threat to this nation's security. What does the INS think he will do – trick innocent Americans into becoming anarchists against their will? . . ."

From the opposite coast of the United States, an editorial in the venerable *Boston Globe* asked:

Farley Mowat, Subversive?

" . . . Mowat did spend a couple of years in the Soviet Union* researching a book on the Siberian people and their relationship to the environment, and he has been friendly with visiting Soviet writers.

"It is also true that some years back Mowat and a couple of friends threatened to steal an atomic bomb from the Strategic Air Command base in Newfoundland and explode it if the United States wouldn't disarm – or, if that didn't work, maybe shoot down some bombers with their .22 rifles.

"Those deeds and misdeeds don't seem all that subversive. What Mowat *has* done is write a book called *Sea of Slaughter*

---

* Actually, two trips, each of six weeks' duration.

in which with both deep feeling and sound documentation, he records the extinction of dozens of species of animal life . . . from Labrador to Cape Cod.

" 'We who are alive today,' Mowat writes, 'can claim no such exculpation [as ignorance] for our biocidal actions and their dire consequences. Modern man has increasing opportunity to be aware of the complexity and interrelationships of the living world. If ignorance is to serve now as an excuse, then it can only be wilful, murderous ignorance.'

"Subversive? it could be – in the eyes of the bureaucratic guardians of our borders."

Back out west, a lady from a town with the fascinating name of Panther Pass sent me a column by Bill Jackson, published in the *Garberville Redwood Record*:

Who do we like?

"Farley Mowat's name attracted my attention when I picked up my first book written by him: *Never Cry Wolf* . . . I remember saying that name out loud to get the full feeling of it. Far-ley Mow-at. When I read *Never Cry Wolf* I entered into what is called Mowat Country. He announced to me the beauty that is the wolf in its natural setting and he wounded me with the undeniable fact that man is the most ruthless animal of all. That quite arbitrary line that we humans draw between ourselves and nature is pierced by Mowat. The way we slaughter so many more animals than we really need is revealed by Mowat. Trophy hunting is exposed for the cruel farce that it really is . . .

"Mowat's twenty-seven books – four of them written for children – all deal with endurance, with man's role among the animals and with his inhumanity to his fellows; . . . In his mind civilized life tends to corrupt; high civilization corrupts absolutely. He is a backwoods moralist. He decries the usurper. And with what we now know about the disaster that awaits humankind if we become too ecologically out of sync, we really need a man like Farley Mowat. He is trying to save us from ourselves . . .

"This week Farley Mowat was denied entry to this country . . . Explanation given: His name is on a list of bad guys. How does one qualify to get on such a list? Explanation given: He is either a communist or an anarchist. No further comment was given by the Department of Immigration. The man is not a communist according to his knowledge or anybody else's. Anarchist is defined as one who rebels against the established order or the ruling power. The ruling power is greed. The established order is based on profit-oriented exploitation of any and all natural resources with total disregard for any ecological considerations. It says somewhere in the Bible that prophets are never welcome in their own land.

"What it all boils down to is this: We live in a country whose president plans to lay wreaths at the graves of the most despicable war criminals that have ever breathed, and whose borders are closed to great writers. Who *do* we like?"

At the risk of appearing unduly chauvinistic, I include some comments from Canada's premier syndicated columnist, Allan Fotheringham, who writes for Southam Press from Washington, D.C.

The Menace of Mowat
"For such a great country, the United States can contain an extraordinary number of twits in official positions.

"For such an ebullient and confident nation, it is surprisingly fearful that it can be contaminated and damaged by such fearful things as ideas.

"This all comes with the news that the international danger, that fearsome threat, Farley Mowat, has been barred from the U.S. of A. because he might put the republic in peril . . .

"It is properly ironic that the nervous Yanks have given him his greatest bit of publicity yet, at a time when Mowat has calmed down from his previous Brendan Behan-ish period when he used to terrorize the Canadian literary circuit.

"The whole thing would be ludicrous . . . if it didn't reveal the nervous underside of this powerful nation.

"We had all assumed the infamous McCarran Act, brought in at the height of the Joe McCarthy era in 1952, was dead and gone. Here it is, still on the books, barring entry to communists, anarchists and like-minded advocates, and used to ban Farley, whose major sin is that his jokes are so broad even an immigration official missed them . . .

"Mowat is a threat only because he has a wild sense of humor. This mighty land is still not mighty sure of itself."

Canadian lawgivers were not to be left out. Member of Parliament Rod Murphy took the opportunity to tell the House of Commons:

"What red-blooded Canadian did not feel there was some nefarious threat or hidden meaning behind books called *The Boat Who Wouldn't Float* or *The Dog Who Wouldn't Be*? The man who wrote those books has been seen talking to unsuspecting school children. He has had courses named after him . . . He has been seen sneaking into Government House.* He has been known to prowl our northern frontiers.

"But now, thanks to the work of the U.S. immigration officials, we are no longer fooled . . . This House owes a vote of thanks to the U.S. Immigration Department . . ."

By the time I finished reading these, I was feeling considerably bucked. I took advantage of the longer intervals between phone calls to read some letters, too. Although not many dealing with my current problems had reached me as yet, those that had were of a quality and nature to make me feel positively exhilarated.

In the interests of "confidentiality," as the INS would put it, I have not appended the authors' names to the excerpts that follow, excepting only those already published. One never knows . . . However, the original letters are available to anyone with the proper security clearance.**

From Solvang, California:

"A group of people in the Santa Ynez Valley (President Reagan votes here) have formed the 'Save Farley Mowat Society' . . . younger members are all for raising funds to

---

* Canada's equivalent to the White House, and the official home of the Governor General of Canada.

** I have included some letters here that were not actually received until some days later, but which had been mailed before April 25.

'coyote' you over the border, but wiser heads prevail . . . It was suggested you claim to be a Chinese communist tennis player, which would secure you immediate admission."

From a medical doctor in Ross, California:

"If our President had any wit or decency, he would sack the functionary who kept you out, have a good laugh over your Air Force One proposition, and invite you for dinner at the White House."

A resident of Menlo Park sent me a copy of this letter to the President:

"My personal FBI and other agency files will verify my record as an anti-communist going back to the 1950s . . . In the battle to influence people's minds worldwide, the action of the INS in denying entry to Canadian writer Farley Mowat is probably worth four or five divisions to the Soviets . . . The INS action is wrong in substance and criminally stupid in propaganda terms . . . Only you, Mr. President, can clean up our act now . . . Mowat is a world resource, and we need him much more than he needs us."

A lawyer in Redding, Connecticut, also wrote to President Reagan, and sent copies to his state representatives:

"I agree with Farley Mowat who thinks it's humorous.

"It is humorous when the United States, seat of democracy, repository of freedom of expression, won't allow an eminent Canadian author to visit our country.

"I also find it humorous that the INS agents of our enlightened democracy are behaving like a bunch of Soviet agents at Moscow airport.

"Not only should Mowat have the right to come to America and express his views, we have the right to hear and know his views . . . I ask that he be granted entry immediately. Moreover, you should apologize to him on behalf of the U.S. government for such shabby treatment.

"Surely on your next visit to Santa Barbara, you could give Farley a lift to the West Coast aboard Air Force One?"

Taking no chances, a lady geographer sent copies of *her* letter to the Embassy of Canada [*sic*], to half-a-dozen U.S. lawgivers, to several newspapers, and to my publishers:

". . . One must wonder if the Immigration Service's zealous protectiveness of us from Mr. Mowat's leftist thinking is real? Or is it perhaps more convenient to muzzle him with the Red herring of communist tendencies . . .

"Most reasonable people will not accept such spurious reasons to bar him . . . He was not coming to persuade us politically, he was coming to tell us what our arrogance toward this planet is costing us . . . Speaking as an American I would personally like to apologize to him."

Not everyone agreed with her, as was evidenced by a letter from Seattle:

"Don't know *accurately* about your entry to the U.S. but I did hear your comments and gestures relative to same. [Probably the writer was referring to the CBC-TV interview, during which I thumbed my nose. CBC reaches Seattle from its Vancouver transmitter.]

"I would be most pleased if you *never* came across the border into our country for *any* reason and I am certain that my Fellow Countrymen and women overwhelmingly agree."

One who did not agree addressed her letter to me through the Prime Minister's Office in Ottawa:

"Imagine the sweet predicament into which you have put this faithful fan! Howinhell did I know, as I sat enjoying your books, that I was probably assisting to overthrow the government of the USA?

"Here I am – a faithful citizen – brush my teeth three times a day, salute the flag, own a gas-guzzling Detroit car, and all of a sudden I'm a bloody traitor!

"I'm holed up in my house awaiting that knock on the door that indicates the INS, CIA, FBI and Book-burners Society have come to get me . . . Enough! Keep the Maple Leaf flying while we try to rescue the Stars and Stripes."

And from a student in Chico:

"Frankly I'm not interested in your politics, and have no knowledge of what they are. I really don't think that this would make any difference to my attitude toward your books. From them, I can't discern anything about your politics, except that you are greatly concerned about saving life on earth; so am I.

"I can't conceive of any way your visit would be as damaging as the President's visit to SS war graves. What an insane world we live in . . ."

A Bible student in Jefferson City, Missouri, wrote briefly, but to the point:

"Please forgive my country. Most of the people in this country aren't as paranoid as the people in Washington. Pray for us."

And a card from Detroit made my day:

"Trying to come up with a reason for refusal to let you in. All can come up with is your book on Russia. Must have been the title that put you on the list as I don't believe the current administration reads anything but Westerns, which isn't necessarily bad, just irresponsible."

Finally, there was a hand-printed letter from a Grade IV girl in Madison, New Jersey:

"I don't think it's fair to stop you coming to visit us. We are all supposed to have the right to speak what we think."

I don't want to give the impression I was fighting my war singlehandedly. The support troops were carrying a lot of the load. From her New York office, publicity manager Susan DiSesa (who told me she had wept with frustration at the cancellation of my tour) was frantically busy trying to orchestrate U.S. media coverage and directing reporters and interviewers to my beleaguered bunker in Port Hope. Her tears had turned to ecstasy as she contemplated the publicity now accruing to *Sea of Slaughter*.

"If only," she pleaded hopefully over the phone, "you would goad Jerry Falwell into demanding that your books be burned on the grounds that you're a Godless atheist who believes we're all descended from monkeys . . ."

"Susan," I said sternly. "Control yourself. You are being greedy."

She apologized and I could forgive her, for she was living a publicist's fantasy.

Jack McClelland continued to do his stuff, concentrating on needling Canadian government officials in Ottawa and Washington until he so exasperated one senior diplomat that, speaking only half in jest I suspect, this mandarin threatened to see that Jack himself was put into the "lookout book."

The prospect delighted Jack. "God, what an honour that

would be! Think of the company I'd be in! Me and Pierre Trudeau, and Graham Greene, and Bertrand Russell and, well yes, you too, Farley."

Peter Davison's overseas contacts advised him that the story was now fully international, having appeared in such papers as the *London Daily Telegraph*, the *London Observer*, the *Paris Tribune*, the *Jerusalem Post*, and, of course, *Izvestia*. Peter was pursuing his own tack through various civil rights organizations rallying support for Congressman Barney Frank's preparations to reintroduce a bill that would at least remove the most odious aspects of the McCarran-Walter Act.

He sent me copies of his correspondence, and I quote from one of his letters to Frank:

"From the point of view of the United States, its ideals and its dedication to the free exchange of ideas, nothing could be more harmful than the idiotic behaviour of the Immigration officials. I am not one who likes to see my country with its pants down in public. The Mowat scandal embarrassed those United States officials who were at that very moment engaged in discussions with Canadian officials in Washington about improving relations. It was an embarrassment to the Canadian government which was forced to intercede for Mowat . . . But most of all it was an embarrassment and a shame that the most distinguished author now writing on Canadian soil should have his preconceptions about the United States confirmed by its official policy . . .

"The instance is silly; the principle is far from silly. Please let me know what we at *The Atlantic*, what I in person, can do to help alter our policy in these matters."

On this day, our private lives seemed to be regaining some semblance of normality. Claire even dared sneak away in the afternoon to her hidden garret in downtown Port Hope, there to work on her new book.

Although I could not escape from the house, and servitude to Ma Bell, there was at least an opportunity to reflect a little on what had taken place since that startling moment on Tuesday morning at Pearson International Airport.

In retrospect, my strongest emotion was one of astonishment amounting almost to incredulity, not at what the INS had done but at the way individuals and even institutions had rallied around. With apprehension almost amounting to panic in that first day, I had expected to have to fight against fearsome, even hopeless odds in my own defence, with precious few allies. It had not turned out that way at all.

As I sifted through the clippings littering my desk, it was clear that the media had never been less than fair, had been scrupulous in obtaining and publishing my point of view, and had, in many cases, come out frankly and overtly on my side. This was true not only of the Canadian media but *especially* of the American media. This seemed almost inexplicable to me, because I had always taken it as an article of faith that U.S. newspapers, magazines, radio, and television were for the most part so staunchly defensive of the American Way of Life that a foreigner who dared make mock of their country, its politics and attitudes, would get scant mercy at their hands.

Yet I had done the unthinkable (was still doing it) and instead of being castigated for it or, worse still, ignored, I was being warmly seconded by many of the most prestigious media voices in America!

More than that; of the numerous telephone calls and telegrams I had received from Americans, hardly any had criticized my stand, although almost all had criticized the actions of their own authorities.

As for the mail, only three of the several hundred letters and cards (mostly from the U.S.A.), which eventually reached me, took me to task. I have already quoted from one and the others will appear in due course.

Late Friday afternoon, a Canadian Press dispatch from Washington carried startling news.

"Author Farley Mowat could be allowed into the United States under provisions that allow a special inquiry to be temporarily waived, a U.S. Immigration officer said today.

"Duke Austin said that Mowat could be allowed into the U.S. immediately, and an inquiry held either at some point in the visit, or afterwards."

The Associated Press carried a more detailed report, which was phoned to me by a staffer on the *New York Times*, although his paper did not carry the story until Saturday.

"The State Department has asked immigration authorities to allow Farley Mowat to enter the United States to promote his latest book, a department official said . . .

"The United States government has said it barred Mr. Mowat from visiting the United States under Federal laws concerning 'membership in proscribed organizations'. Officials refuse to identify the organization or organizations.

"Asked if Mr. Mowat was being punished for his views as a member of Canada's small, liberal New Democratic Party, department officials declined to respond.

"But asked if the [State] department had requested immigration officials to allow Mr. Mowat into the country, an official who demanded anonymity said, 'Yes'.

"While Attorney General Edwin Meese III has the final decision on allowing Mowat in, it would be unusual for the Justice Department, the parent organization of the INS, not to accede to State Department wishes."

"Not before effing time!" was Jack's comment when I reported this news to him. "But you ain't in yet, so don't count your chickens. I'll check it out with Ottawa."

When he called back, it was to tell me that the offer was official. "External knows about it and is surprised you don't. They say the American Ambassador promised to notify you himself last night. But you know him!"

Indeed I did. Ambassador Paul H. Robinson, Jr., had obtained the job because of his success as a political fund-raiser. He had distinguished himself during his tenure in Ottawa by publicly treating Canada like a banana republic, frequently ticking us off for failing to hew more closely to the Reagan line. I had met him at an official function in Ottawa and had not found him endearing. I suspect the reaction was mutual.

Peter Davison's enthusiasm was muted when he heard the news. He pointed out that even if I were to be admitted now, it was too late to reschedule the promotion tour. "If what they really had in mind was to scuttle it, then they've succeeded."

Still and all, I was elated by this whiff of victory, even though it might turn out to be Pyrrhic.

Claire took some of the pleasure out of the moment by inquiring what I would have been doing on this Friday evening had all gone according to plan.

I would have been in Chico.

At 7:00 p.m., I would have been sitting in the university theatre watching Charlie Martin-Smith play me, in *Never Cry Wolf*; Farley Martin-Smith, as he had become in a mockserious adoptive ceremony on the movie location in the Yukon, where I had become Charlie Mowat.

I wondered whether or not the evening's program had been cancelled. Probably; and I was distressed to think that I had failed Michael Bauman, even through no fault of mine. As it turned out, I had not entirely failed him. While we were eating dinner in Port Hope that evening, Chico was experiencing "An Evening Without Farley Mowat." Michael told me about it in a letter written the next day.

"How high indignation has been running in Chico may be reflected in the turnout to our showing of *Never Cry Wolf*. After. it, we showed *In Search of Farley Mowat*, a lovely, honest film that, luckily, I had gotten hold of before the storm broke and which allowed us to see you right before us and get to know you a little.* The auditorium was packed [with] students, faculty, librarians, townspeople. I read them the enclosed note to you and said that anyone who wished might sign it . . .

"People keep asking me whether or not you'll be coming in the future . . . my wife and I wish you all the best; we love your books and the things you stand for, and the way you stand for them. Today, we thank you for teaching the world by personal example that governments are *not* machines but people and that, as such, governments had better learn to have a sense of humour if they wish to be humane in fact, not merely in fiction."

Michael's appended note read simply:

"Dear Farley Mowat:

"We, the undersigned, deplore our government's action –

---

* An hour-long documentary made in 1981 by the National Film Board of Canada.

and apologize. We'll do *our* best to make Air Force One pick you up in Toronto and fly you out to California!

"Yours most sincerely . . ."

It bore 108 signatures.

Reproduced courtesy the *Casper Star-Tribune*, Casper, Wyoming.

V

Saturday and Sunday, April 27-28

We've left the weekend flexible. If the weather's good, and it almost always is, we could take you up into the Sierras, maybe to Lassen Volcanic National Park one day, and the other make a canoe trip on the Sacramento. Nobody is going to hassle you. If you'd rather just sit in the sun with a cool drink and rap or even snooze that will be okay too . . .

Snoozing in the sun would have been fine with me that morning but, alas, it was not to be. The imperious demands of the phone began again shortly after 7:00 a.m. The first caller was from the Washington bureau of the Canadian Press. He wanted to know how I felt now that I was free to enter the United States.

"Nobody's told *me* I'm free to do that."

"The U.S. authorities haven't been in touch?"

"They haven't been in touch since this whole thing started," I said with some acerbity. "They've said plenty to the press, but not one damn word to me personally. Why should they start showing common courtesy at this late stage in the game?"

"Why indeed?" he soothed me. "Then let me be the first to tell you . . ."

The CP dispatch that went across Canada that morning ran as follows:

"Author Farley Mowat will be allowed to enter the United States . . . under an agreement reached Friday, a U.S. immigration spokesman said.

"The agreement, which capped three days of diplomatic

maneuvering by Canadian and U.S. officials, wipes out an earlier U.S. demand that Mowat appear at a U.S. entry point to have his case reviewed . . ."

" 'In the interests of international harmony, we are permitting Mr. Mowat to come to the United States to complete his business,' said the INS statement . . . [but] Immigration spokesman Duke Austin said the agreement does not mean Mowat's name has been removed from the so-called Lookout Book . . . 'The grounds under which he was deemed inadmissibile still remain in his file,' Austin said . . .

"A senior State Department official, citing foreign policy [as a reason], asked INS officials Thursday to 'drop' their objections to Mowat's entry. Canadian officials had vigorously protested Mowat's treatment . . .

"The controversy, which has received prominent attention in the U.S. media, has set off initial rumblings on Capitol Hill against the current immigration laws . . ."

"You going to take them up on it?" the reporter asked.

"I don't know, but I likely won't if they're keeping me in their Black Book. I'll let you know what my plans are when the fog thins out a bit."

A short time later, a call from George Lardner, Jr., at the *Washington Post* clarified the situation. Lardner had braced the INS, demanding to know precisely what the terms governing my entry were. Here are the relevant *Post* excerpts.

"The INS has offered Farley Mowat a 'parole' to come to the United States . . . but Mowat quickly rejected the offer, calling it 'totally unacceptable'.

" 'I want total clearance or nothing,' Mowat said in a telephone interview from his home in Port Hope, Ontario. 'Parole! My God, it sounds like I'm a criminal. I wouldn't touch it with a ten-foot pole!'

"INS Commissioner Alan C. Nelson said the offer, which officials acknowledged was limited, was being made 'in the interests of international harmony' after requests from the Canadian government and consultations with the State Department. But Immigration officials also said Mowat would be halted at the border if he tries to make another trip. 'When we parole somebody, what we're saying is, you have a right to move about the United States, but you haven't been *ad-*

mitted,' INS spokesman Duke Austin said. 'The conditions which were deemed to make him inadmissible have not been resolved.' . . .

"The carefully-worded INS statement emphasized that Mowat could 'come' to the United States 'for the purpose of completing his business,' . . . Austin said the word 'come' was used because 'enter' has a 'legal connotation which our people are very sensitive about.' Mowat's name, Austin added, will remain in the 'Lookout Book' . . .

"Mowat replied that he would, 'in the interests of international harmony,' forget about having an apology delivered by Air Force One and would settle for 'unencumbered permission to cross the American border . . . if I'm not granted this, I will remain in my native land, and shed no tears'."

Canadian Press and United Press International duly reported my reactions, having toned them down somewhat to make them editorially palatable.

"Mowat says he will 'stay in his own sweet country' rather than agree to entering the United States under the agreement reached by the U.S. officials," said Canadian Press. But what I had *actually* said (approximately) was "There is no effing way I'll go to the States on terms like that! The bastards are just trying to turn off the heat – trying to con you guys and everyone else into thinking everything is now hunky-dory. Kiss and make up! If the *Post* hadn't squeezed their knockers, they might have gotten away with it too! God Almighty but they're a slippery lot!"

The *Sacramento Bee* was not as circumspect as her media sisters. It reported my response as: "There is no bloody way!" The *Chicago Tribune*'s Janet Crawley gave my reason for rejecting the INS offer in sanitized form. "It's a one-shot deal for a single visit only. It's obviously intended to quiet the ruckus; and I'm not buying it."

When I got through fuming at this transparent scam, I took a harder look at the newspeak and bafflegab with which it had been cloaked. And I was bewildered. Nor was I the only one, as is evidenced by a letter published in the *Washington Post* a few days later.

"When dictators or bureaucrats want to use words the

(

meaning of which they don't approve, they solve the problem by changing the definition.

"The case of Farley Mowat . . . provides a classic example.

"To explain how the INS could admit Mr. Mowat without admitting that they were admitting him, Duke Austin, INS spokesman, said they would 'parole' him. *Parole* him? Mr. Duke explained: 'When we parole somebody, what we're saying is you have a right to move about the United States, but you haven't been *admitted*.' . . .

"Mr. Mowat must feel that he has fallen down Alice's rabbit hole and is dealing with the Mad Hatter, the Queen of Hearts, or Tweedledum. What a shame that bureaucrats have made our country such a Wonderland."

My decision not to let U.S. officialdom slip off the hook upon which it had skewered itself was not universally approved. Jack called to tell me that Ottawa was in a snit. "They think you're being bull-headed. 'Why isn't he satisfied?' they asked me. So I told them if they had to ask an asinine question like that, they didn't deserve an answer."

"External's maybe hoping for some credit," I said, "but I doubt they had that much input – who the hell listens to them in Washington? More to the point, I had a chat this morning with a charming-sounding lady from the Cherry-blossom city itself. Said she is a Mowat fan and, while she's no Deep Throat, she did volunteer she once worked for State. She said I wouldn't *believe* the amount of mail that's come in there, *and* to the White House, *and* to Congress and the Senate, raising the devil about the Mowat hassle. She said if she had a dollar for every letter, she'd buy me a nice little country of my own and guarantee me uncontested entry."

Jack chuckled lewdly. "Well, anyhow, you've made the right decision. Don't give an effing inch."

Despite his reassurance, I worried that my refusal to accept the INS offer might be interpreted either as sheer obstinacy or as a deliberate ploy aimed at keeping the story alive for the sake of the publicity *Sea of Slaughter* would continue to receive. However, nothing materialized to suggest that this apprehension was justified. To the contrary, support for my cause seemed to intensify.

Typical of continuing Canadian reaction was an editorial in the *Edmonton Journal*.

The Mowat Mystery

"Celebrities, remote rendezvous, innuendo and international intrigue – Farley Mowat's experiences this week had all the ingredients for a best-selling spy thriller . . .

"An official in Washington . . . said Mowat was denied entry because he belongs to an outlawed organization. Could this have been the dreaded Order of Canada – a foreign society which, at least for now, is beyond Washington's control? . . .

"Why did the U.S. *really* deny Mowat entry? Maybe it felt threatened because he's an *outspoken* Canadian . . . Perhaps the Americans were afraid Mowat's books will make people even more concerned about the preservation of wildlife and man's coexistence with nature . . ."

In the United States, the tone grew increasingly cutting, as witness these excerpts from an editorial in the conservative *Chicago Tribune*.

The Author and the Airheads

"Said Canadian author Farley Mowat: 'I'm beginning to think there are some people in your State Department that don't have any sense of humour'. The last two words are unnecessary. The immigration officers who barred Mr. Mowat from the United States must have undergone a brain bypass.

". . . On Tuesday . . . INS officials stopped [Mr. Mowat]; it seems his name was on their 'lookout book', a list of inadmissible aliens.

"Mr. Mowat is a bluntly independent writer who has spent much of his life battling bureaucrats. The INS has given him and every other Canadian a fat target; and they and the rest of the U.S. government can expect to be savagely lampooned. The airheads responsible for the exclusion order deserve it. But do we deserve them?"

Some of the most telling salvos fired during the weekend came not from major newspapers in great U.S. cities but from the hinterland. I offer two examples. The first was written by Steve Lachowicz in the *Wenatchee World*, Wenatchee, Washington:

Government Tells Us What To Think!

"The most deeply disturbing news article of the week was not about Nicaragua, nor about the federal budget deficit . . . The most troubling story was about gagging free speech and smothering ideas in the one country which is supposed to stand most staunchly, in all the world, for precisely the opposite.

"Ours.

"The U.S. Immigration Service blocked Canadian author Farley Mowat from entering the United States . . . Even though immigration backed down on its ban later in the week under pressure . . . the damage was done.

"Since when is the U.S. government in the business of deciding what views are acceptable for Americans to be exposed to? Mowat's books . . . are freely available here . . . *Never Cry Wolf* was even turned into a successful motion picture . . . the film came from those well-known communists and anarchists, the Disney Studios.

"A major U.S. television network even did a prime-time movie a few years ago based on another work of Mowat's, *A Whale for the Killing* . . . What possible sense does it make to prevent an author of such works from sharing his insights in person, instead of just on the printed page or on film?

"Immigration's action . . . stands as a warning to all of us. It is an incident in which we find our own government deciding for us what it is good to listen to, or talk about. This censorship is as objectionable and repressive as anything we so frequently accuse the Russians, or the Cubans or the Chinese of doing.

"There is a wonderful anthology of selections from Mowat's works titled *The World of Farley Mowat* collected and edited by Peter Davison. In his introduction, Davison wrote . . .

" 'It is the 'natural' order, in which man lives in harmony with his surroundings, that Mowat finds to characterize the Golden Age – no age that ever was on sea or land, but an age that can blossom into being at any time . . .

" 'Mowat's books all deal with endurance, with man's role among the animals and with his inhumanity to his fellows; and they give as much attention to the victims of inhumanity as to man's ability to survive long enough for laughter . . .

" 'In one book after another we hear his favourite words – existence, elemental, irresistible, struggle – repeating themselves in the rhythm of insistence on what it is that holds us together in the companionship of animals. It is part of being animals that enables us to feel the tie . . . between the dying whale and her sentinel at the edge of the sea, between husband and wife, between a son and his father, a boy and his dog, even between a writer and his friends. We do not survive in order to die as victims, but to live as companions.' "

Although it may be a trifle narcissistic to quote someone quoting someone else on the subject of myself, I plead in extenuation that I could hardly express those sentiments as well in my own words.

The second piece, by Charles Levendosky, appeared in the *Star-Tribune* of Casper, Wyoming, and in four other Wyoming newspapers:

Freedom of Speech On Parole In America
"Farley Mowat, the Canadian author who was stopped from entering the United States . . . is being paroled-in to the United States in the interests of international harmony, according to Duke Austin of the INS.

" 'Paroled-in' gives the right flavour. INS officials obviously still think Mowat is a criminal of some kind – an ideological criminal. Apparently Reagan's America must be protected from a writer who has visited Russia to write a book, who writes books about environmental issues, who joins the New Democratic Party, and once joked about shooting a U.S. bomber out of Canadian airspace with a .22-calibre rifle . . .

"Mowat has wisely refused the INS one-time-only special to be 'paroled into America' . . . Mowat knows that his name will remain in the INS 'Lookout Book' . . .

"The 'Lookout Book' lists 40,000 foreigners who might be, under the McCarran-Walter Act, considered undesirables. The list is not compiled by the CIA, but by immigration officials. From what sources these suspicions are documented, Benedict Ferro, the district director of immigration with jurisdiction in Mowat's case, would not say. Presumably this is classified information.

"The list of names is also classified information and cannot be released even under the Freedom of Information Act. And District Director Ferro would not reveal which violations of the McCarran-Walter Act Farley Mowat is accused of committing. 'In order to protect Mr. Mowat's privacy', was the way he put it.

"The concern for Mowat's privacy is touching, if ironic. Now the entire world knows that immigration officials denied one of Canada's most prominent writers entry into the United States . . . The 'respect for privacy' cuts both ways, often to the detriment of the individual challenged . . . 'Respect for privacy' may save the INS embarrassment, at the expense of the dignity [and, Levendosky might have added, reputation] of the person involved. It allows nameless officials and bureaucrats to hide behind walls of secrecy.

"District Director Ferro: 'Our officers at Toronto advised Mr. Mowat that in order to complete his inspection, in order to go forward with his inspection, he would either have to have a hearing or he would have to go to Buffalo, to the Peace Bridge in Buffalo where we would further develop some of the areas of concern that we have. They did not specifically advise him what areas of concern because all they have access to there was the notice that the agency [INS] did have, in fact, a file which had information which we wished to pursue further with him.'*

"Is that enough bureaucratic jargon? Remember Franz Kafka? The pervasive sense of guilt? The underlying assumption is that Farley Mowat is guilty until proven innocent . . .

"At 63 years of age, Mowat is probably the most honoured Canadian author . . . [there follows a long encomium which we can do without].

"This is the calibre of man who was stopped. This is the calibre of man who is now offered 'parole' into the United States. No wonder he turned it down.

---

* As I have said in the opening chapter, the INS officers in Toronto gave me no such advice – in fact, no advice at all!

"Canadian writers are as shocked and angry as I am, as many Americans are. Canadian novelist David McFadden spoke of the 'incredible anti-communist paranoia which is just destroying the United States'. Perhaps Toronto poet Greg Gatenby expressed it best . . . when he said: 'There is more genuine anger than surprise [in Mowat's rejection] . . . you can't believe the disbelief with which we are regarding the United States . . . and [then there is] the whole Central America situation . . . it's like watching your brother become an alcoholic . . . a mixture of sadness and amazement, as there is no help we can give.'

"He's right – we are addicted to bottle after bottle of anti-communism. Sadly, our immigration officers sip at the Mc-Carran Act and will do so until it is repealed or replaced. Only then will a country which glories in its constitutional right of freedom give more than drunken, slurred lip service to this ideal."

Lest I give the impression that the tyranny of the telephone had let up as the week ended, I find that I logged thirty calls on Saturday, including interviews with all three major U.S. commercial radio networks.

By Saturday evening, Claire and I, enthusiastically seconded by the two dogs, concluded we had had enough for the nonce. So Claire packed a food hamper and I paroled us all to our rough-hewn cabin where the telephone has yet to follow.

It was a chill evening so I lit a fire in the wood stove and, after we had eaten, we listened to some Bach concertos on the battery radio before trundling off to bed.

After what we had endured during the past five days the silence seemed almost eerie – yet marvellously soothing. I wondered if one would feel like this in the High Sierra country overlooking Chico and decided that one probably would. A deer mouse skittered across the floor under our bed and I slipped into sleep, more welcome because it was almost dreamless.

I had intended to devote Sunday to bird-watching in the surrounding fields and woods, but it rained from dawn till dusk. No matter. I saw occasional flashes of colour against the rain-curtain beyond the window and knew that the spring warblers had come back. And an olive-backed thrush, his vibrant mood undampened, sang his rich roundelay at intervals throughout the day.

There being nothing more demanding to do that afternoon, I sprawled on an old couch under the low south window and idly re-read one of Harold Horwood's books about animal life in Newfoundland. Without invitation, both black dogs joined me on the couch. A singularly pleasant smell titillated our nostrils as Claire simmered the ingredients for a robust stew.

After a while, I drifted into a Newfoundland reverie . . . remembering wading along the beaches of Conception Bay amongst millions of spawning capelin . . . watching fin whales sporting off the south coast . . . sailing our schooner into the fogs of St. Pierre . . .

Suddenly both dogs sat bolt upright, ears cocked and noses quivering. In a moment I became aware of the approach of a cataract of thunderous sound, fiercely invading our solitude. The dogs leapt down and galloped for the door. I followed on their heels.

"What in bloody hell is that?" I shouted at Claire, raising my voice to its maximum in order to be heard. She only shook her head. As I plunged out the door into the drizzle, the noise became so overwhelming that I pressed both hands to my ears . . . and looked up.

An enormous aircraft swept past through the grey scud not more than a few hundred feet above the cabin roof. It shook me with its battering discord, then vanished into the murk again.

Scrambling back inside, I fixed my wife with a look of wild surmise.

"That was a 707 – I'll swear to it! You don't suppose . . .?"

She brought me back to earth as only she can do.

"Calm down, Farley. It's only the air force transport pilots practising from Trenton Air Force Base. You know it's only ten miles away as the crow – as the jet flies. If you're thinking what I'm sure you are . . . forget it. Sit down and have your stew."

Why, oh why, must women be so often right?

VI

Monday and Tuesday, April 29 and 30

Michael Bauman will drive you to the airport Sunday:
Depart Sacramento 6:30 p.m. Samoan Airlines #709.
Arrive San Francisco 7:20 p.m.
Harry Collins, Little Brown sales rep. will pick you up at
the airport and drive you to the Stanford Court Hotel. Harry
will be your escort in the San Francisco region. Your schedule
will include:
San Francisco Chronicle, exclusive interview
News Magazine, KCBS-Radio
New Dimensions, Radio
People Are Talking, KPIX-TV
Joel Spivak Show, KNBR-Radio
Weekend Update, KRON-TV
A number of bookstore visits and autographings, including
the Nature Company Bookstore.

Rain or not, Sunday had done all of us a lot of good, especially me. A day divorced from the idiocies and artifices of the man-made world had much improved my digestion, if not my disposition. I was again in touch with the verities, and the border incident had ceased to engage my full attention.

It came back into centre focus within an hour of our arrival home on Monday morning, when barking dogs heralded the arrival at our door of a uniformed courier. He handed me an envelope emblazoned in large blue letters to the effect that this was *The United States of America* on *Official Business*.

My first thought was that it must be from the hand of Ambassador Robinson, but no, the envelope carried only the insignia of the U.S. Consulate in Toronto. It was dated Friday,

April 26th, from which I calculated that, in its peregrinations along the sixty-odd miles of highway lying between the Consulate and my home, it had averaged no better than twenty miles a day. Yet I am nearly certain the courier was driving a motor vehicle, not a pony cart.

Never mind. At *last* I was in possession of an Official Communication. I ripped open the envelope with the anticipation of a child on Christmas morning.

Dear Mr. Mowat:
    I would like to inform you that the U.S. Immigration and Naturalization Service has authorized your entry into the United States under the provisions of the Immigration and Nationality Act for the month-long [*sic*] promotional tour which has been arranged by your publisher. I hope this delay will not complicate your scheduled business activity in the United States.
    I understand that you will depart from Canada by air from Toronto. I would appreciate it if you would let me know the timing of your departure so that I might inform the INS officials at the airport. In that connection, I recommend that you have this letter available for presentation should it be necessary.
    Please let me know if I may be of any further assistance in this matter.
Sincerely,

J. Donald Blevins
Consul General

J. Donald Blevins was certainly laying out the old welcome mat! My stomach began to rumble once again.

I sat down to compose a reply and, after throwing the first several drafts into the toilet adjoining to my office (they might have ignited spontaneously in the wastepaper basket), I produced this oh-so-cool reply:

Dear Mr. Blevins:
    Thank you for your letter, which was only delivered to me this morning, and which constitutes the first communi-

cation I have received from an official of the United States of America.

Unfortunately it does not contain any reference to the conditions specified by the INS spokesman in Washington, that I am to be permitted entry into the USA only on a "one shot" basis; nor does it mention that I am only to be permitted entry under the parole section of the relevant INS regulations.

Needless to say, these restrictions are totally unacceptable to me. I might also point out that the INS action has so disrupted my tour that it would now be virtually impossible to reconstitute it . . .

May I please be informed of the procedure by which I may obtain a copy of my so-called file, said to contain the reasons why I was excluded from the United States.

Would you also be good enough to clarify the entry conditions. For example, am I at liberty to enter at any time and place of my own choosing . . . ?

Taken by and large, this was a lousy letter, whose overblown verbiage indicated that I might have become infected with Bureaucratese myself. I wish now that I had sent my first draft. Perhaps the original sizzler would have had more effect, since nobody replied to the one I *did* send. But then again, maybe Donald did reply . . . and it still hasn't reached me.

So began, and so ended, direct communications between me and my cementhead adversaries.

Claire took the taste of Blevins' letter away by bringing me a mug of fresh tea. As I sipped it, she came back into my work room with a strange expression on her face.

"I've just been riffling through the newspaper from last week, Farley. I know you scoff at things like this, but have a look. It's your horoscope for Tuesday, the day of your departure for the States."

I grunted but took the proffered sheet. I could hardly believe what I was reading. Claire had underlined these words in red: "Now is the time for you to move to centre stage . . ."

I looked up at her grinning face. We giggled, whinnied, and were close to hysterics in a bout of mirth that must have lasted a quarter of an hour.

"Okay, love," I said when we had finally sobered up. "You've convinced me about horoscopes. I will call an astrologer right away and find out what the INS has got against me. It is likely the only way we will ever get to know."

Only a handful of media inquiries disturbed this day, and their calls were to become fewer with each day that followed. The INS offer to let me come to the U.S.A. had effectively achieved its purpose. The duel between David and Goliath appeared to have ended in victory for the underdog. That this was a non-event, contrived to give the illusion of reality, did not signify. The story had run its course, and so it passed out of the news columns and disappeared from the newscasts.

Not before time, as far as I personally was concerned. Although our brief escape to the cabin had eased some of the tensions, I was exhausted, and willing enough to see the battle end even, as it appeared to have done, in this rather inconclusive fashion. However, although the clamour of hand-to-hand combat was fading, big guns behind the lines continued to roar.

"Affront to Canada" was the heading of an editorial in the *Kansas City Star*:

"The U.S. government's reaction to a possible visit by the distinguished Canadian author Farley Mowat is embarrassing. Some attempt to recoup lost face should be made at once, and apologies extended.

"Mr. Mowat . . . was refused entry because he showed up on a list of 40,000 foreigners deemed by the government as undesirables. What numbskull makes up this list? The government used provisions of the McCarran Act, a law passed at the height of McCarthyism in 1952 to keep out communists and other trouble-makers, to deny his visit. Canadian authorities got hot and protested. The United States gave in and said Mr. Mowat could visit, with restrictions. That may not be enough. At the least Mr. Mowat should be allowed to visit the country on an unrestricted basis . . . The incident regrettably has marred cordial relations with an important ally to the north, and made the U.S. government look stupid."

The *Los Angeles Times* fired an editorial headed "Silly Barriers At The Border":

"The anti-communist hysteria that swept the United States in the 1950s has long since abated, but a vestigial remnant still exists in the immigration laws . . . The latest victim of [these] laws is Farley Mowat, Canadian author and environmentalist . . .

"An unidentified source close to the Immigration and Naturalization Service has reportedly said that Mowat was barred in part because of a newspaper article . . . in 1968 in which he claimed to have fired a rifle at an airplane of the U.S. Strategic Air Command. In response, Mowat told the *New York Times* 'There are some people in your State Department that don't have any sense of humor'. As to his politics, Mowat told National Public Radio, 'I have a lot of communist friends. At least I assume they're communists. I've never asked them.'

"Isn't it obvious that this man poses no threat to this country or to anyone here? By no stretch of the imagination could his appearance on talk shows be expected to incite an insurrection or civil disorder . . . Keeping him out makes this country look silly, and serves no purpose."

The *Washington Post* struck at the heart of the matter:

Time to Get Rid of The McCarran Act

"They've done it again. Early last week U.S. government officials, citing the 1952 McCarran Act, refused to allow a visitor into the United States on political grounds.

"Usually these decisions are made by the State Department, which has the power to deny visas to persons whose presence here is deemed 'prejudicial to the public interest' or dangerous to the 'welfare, safety or security of the United States'.

"This time – because Canadians don't need visas – it was the Immigration and Naturalization Service that stopped writer Farley Mowat . . .

"The McCarran Act was a piece of xenophobic legislation enacted in the early 1950s whose guiding emotion was fear – fear that the wrong people would get into this country and overwhelm or subvert us.

"Its provisions are regularly invoked to keep people out of the country who might say something the government is afraid to have us hear. The act gave broad powers to the bureaucracy to exclude would-be visitors.

"The statute reflects a profound misunderstanding of American free-speech traditions and sadly underestimates the critical judgment of a free people.

"Farley Mowat is a Canadian who writes about the wilderness . . . His latest work is about wildlife on the seacoasts of the United States and Canada. He may have made comments about American military power and may have joined a committee in support of Castro's Cuban government many years ago.

"So what? Surely he does not belong on any list, book or computer file of persons who pose a danger to the country.

"How do these lists get compiled anyway? The State and Justice Departments won't say, but once you're listed, you're there to stay unless the attorney general gives you a special entry waiver every time you want to come into the United States.

"The fact that Mowat was granted a waiver [*sic*] does not solve the general problem. An unknown number of others are on those lists, some because of affiliations or activities that took place decades ago.

"The law is preposterous and outmoded. A country as strong, stable and free as ours can hear Mowat, Nicaraguan Cabinet members (cultural affairs minister Ernesto Cardenal is still waiting for a required waiver), Chinese party leaders, the Rev. Ian Paisley and even Mikhail Gorbachev without falling under their spell.

"Rep. Barney Frank, D-Mass., is planning to introduce legislation to change this law, and his effort deserves support. These offensive restrictions should be repealed."

My favourite was this one, from Tuesday's *Baltimore Sun*:

"Farley Mowat is dangerous. He is pro-wolf, pro-seal and pro-deer. Among humans he is pro-Eskimo, pro-Viking and pro-Siberian. His politics are Newfoundland-revanchist. He has admitted to fear in wartime.

"Worse, this man is a writer. His weapons are words. They cross boundaries, evade radar, and can be shot down only by better words, of which there are few. Sometimes they become images on film and penetrate where even words will not go.

Among his many Canadian and literary awards is the Stephen Leacock Medal for Humour – the ultimate weapon, for which no defence is known.

"Small wonder the INS proscribed him as one of the 40,000 dangerous characters in its 'Lookout Book', to be kept out of the country at all costs under the 1952 McCarran Act. If he were a terrorist, Communist, Nazi or cocaine dealer – all a dime a dozen – INS could afford to look the other way. But this man is a *writer* . . .

"Fortunately the INS caught him red-handed with an airline ticket in Toronto Airport, and banned him . . . Never mind the friendship between Canada and the United States, the greatest free movement of goods and capital and people between two countries in the history of the world. Never mind the unfavourable publicity for the United States. Never mind the ridicule heaped on the Reagan administration ('S.S. troops were victims; seals are killers.').

"You might almost suspect the Commies had penetrated the INS for it to come up with such a harmful move to U.S. interests. Or that his publisher had. It couldn't buy this amount of publicity. But if we let such a man into the country, he would probably try to save the rockfish. He is beyond redemption."

Most of these editorials were reprinted, none more extensively than the *Sun*'s, but I don't want to give the impression that the U.S. press *en masse* was lending its support to my case. Many large-circulation newspapers (and a lot of small ones) whose owners lean toward the Reaganauts and the New Right either gave the incident no play at all or played it down. One can appreciate their reasons. It was not the sort of story to make their political viewpoint seem attractive to people for whom freedom is of much concern.

It seems that the more we rely on the electronic magicians, the worse the mail services become. In Canada, where, not long since, a letter took only two or three days to cross the country, now, despite the aid of an enormous array of new electronic devices, it takes two to three weeks. I understand that the American postal system has been similarly improved.

Thanks to this technological leap forward, it was not until

Monday that the floodgates really opened, deluging me with letters from all over North America, but especially from the U.S.A. Monday morning's massive mail demonstrated that, if my border problem was no longer front-page news, it remained a matter of moment to many U.S. citizens.

I was contemplating the new pile of letters that arrived on Tuesday when Peter Davison called from Richmond, Virginia, where he was about to preside over a book-and-author dinner. "You'd be surprised how many people here have spoken to me about the border incident already," he told me. "Even the Richmond paper had a piece about it. Senator Gary Hart of Colorado and Senator William Cohen of Maine are going to be here tonight, and I'll take the opportunity to bend their ears. Also, I've been in touch with Congressman Barney Frank's office. He's just about to introduce his new bill to amend the McCarran Act, and I think he'll be using a lot of material about your case. How are things going up your way?"

"Well," I said, "something odd is happening. There's been a bunch more news stories and a rash of editorials – all taking our side. But something else is going on that I find more than passing strange."

"Strange? How strange?"

Over the years we'd known each other, Peter and I had differed, sometimes strenuously, about my attitudes toward the U.S.A. Although he is one American who seems to know, and care, something about Canada, he had found my fiery criticisms of U.S. policies abroad trying. Some of the things I railed at as symptomatic of American imperialism, he tended to excuse as the natural requirements of nationalism. And it pained him that I tended to see Americans *en masse* in an antagonistic light. I'm sure he anticipated, with some defensiveness, that the border *imbroglio* would reinforce my critical attitudes. Yet what I had to tell him now was, in a beginning sense at least, a contradiction of my usual self. It wasn't going to be easy.

"Peter," I began, "I'm getting letters. Hundreds of them. From all across the States. And you know what?"

"They all hate you, and say you ought to stay at home, you dubious character."

"No, me son. The strange thing is . . . I was expecting a

pile of anti-Mowat mail . . . but . . . they're all sympathetic! Almost without exception!"

"You're surprised?" Peter asked. "Nobody down here has claimed you were excluded because you're a Canadian rebel, only because you had some ideas in your head. And in your books. And were disrespectful as all hell toward the leadership of the free world. God knows why."

Peter's irony can be a little heavy on occasion.

"Listen, you supercilious bastard, you've missed the point, as usual. When mail from *ordinary* Americans – you don't mind the term? – started pouring in I *expected* it to be mostly hostile. All that stuff about shooting at SAC bombers . . . and thumbing my nose, figuratively and literally, at the big eagle . . . But no, they're on my *side*! Mostly they seem to see the whole shemozzle as a matter of free speech, and as endangering *American* freedom. What do you make of that?"

"It doesn't surprise me a bit. You are the natural enemy of the bureaucrat, and nobody likes to see the double-talkers of this world win a round. That's why you did well on the *Today Show* with Mr. Ferro. You talked English and made sense. He talked officialese, and didn't."

"Yeah. Well, I still find it most peculiar – but *good*, my friend. But *good!*"

After Peter had hung up I pondered for a while over what all this might mean. It was probably too early to be sure. I decided to see what lay buried in Tuesday's crop of State-side letters.

The small mountain of envelopes piled on my desk contained not only many more "favourable" letters, but copies of others sent to newspapers, to President Reagan, and to assorted senators and congressmen representing almost every state in the union. Many were fat with newspaper clippings, without which (as I have already acknowledged but wish to emphasize) it would hardly have been possible to put this book together.

The flood continued through succeeding days, but the import and the impact remained the same. Obviously I can't print all the letters I received, but it is at least incumbent on me to include excerpts from a representative selection, for their authors constitute an authentic and, we must hope, potent component in the sometimes strident, often discordant, and frequently frightening welter of voices that speak, or claim to speak, for America.

As I did earlier, and for the same reasons, I have accorded the writers anonymity.

Hadley, Virginia

Believe me, Mr. Mowat, we had a nice little country going here for a while; we really did.

But what the hell, nothing lasts forever.

A lot of us are pretty ashamed of the fatherland these days, but it seems to be getting almost impossible to put on the brakes. As it says in the old Bob Dylan song: "The vandals took the handles".

For what it's worth I tender, in the name of my beleaguered country, apologies.

Wenatchee, Washington

In closing I would like to apologize to you . . . for the treatment given to you by some bureaucratic asshole whose actions have caused an incident that is definitely embarrassing and mortifying to those of us with an intellect above that of a bivalve.

Richmond, Virginia (to President Reagan)

It is outrageous that Farley Mowat has been denied entrance to the United States. This is tyranny of the first order. What country are we living in, the USA or the Soviet Union? . . . Perhaps you would like to remove all his books from all public and school libraries while you are at it . . .

Jefferson City, Missouri (to Benedict Ferro)

You might find it useful to compare Farley Mowat's sense of humour in the reputed incident of shooting at a U.S. bomber, with Mr. Reagan's "joke" about atom bombing Russia.

Mt. Vernon, Maine

May I apologize for a President who can't, for an Immigration Service that won't, and for a State Department that

confuses humour and humbug with fact. What used to be
Foggy Bottom, and a reasonable source of humour, is now
Disneyland-on-the-Potomac and scary as all hell, especially
to those it used to govern.

Flint, Michigan
I usually don't write letters to people who don't have the
time to read them. However, after reading in the Flint *Journal* about your treatment by my government I wanted to say
how sorry I was. It is depressing, but I know my government
is becoming notorious for this sort of thing. Apparently McCarthyism is alive and well in the United States. . . . The article stated you would not visit the U.S.A. until Air Force One
flew in to pick you up. I hope you are not holding your
breath.

Carson City, Nevada
I am a native born citizen of the United States of America
and I love my country, but I am outraged at what they are
trying to do to you . . .
I only discovered your books about a year ago . . . I wish I
knew what I could do to help.

Cambridge, Massachusetts (published letter to the editor of
the *Boston Globe*)
I am deeply disturbed by our government's exclusion of
Canadian writer Farley Mowat. I understand that the United
States is a land where people come to seek liberty and justice
for all.
People come to the United States to gain the right to have
different religious beliefs and people come . . . to enjoy the
right to be outspoken.
In this case we have an outspoken Canadian wishing to
publicize his newest book and he is told he cannot enter this
country. How can we be true to our Constitution if we say
this?

Amanda Burling

(Eighth Grade
Carroll School)

Arlington, Virginia
Do you know how many writers our free country keeps out due to some prejudice or another? So don't give in. But don't stop trying either. It goes beyond you. And besides, none of your readers down here are one bit scared of you!

New Orleans, Louisiana
I thought, Mr. Mowat, for all the world that I was watching some surrealistic bit of comedy [on the *Today Show*] as that twit in Buffalo spouted his perfectly meaningless bureaucratese at you. But there is a chill behind the humour of the absurd. As Calvin Trillin said recently, the Reagan administration so defies the imagination, and boggles the mind that its antics have almost rendered the satirist redundant and obsolete . . . I humbly apologize as an American to you, for this silly yet ugly incident.

Worcester, Vermont
I have never found anything offensive or "dangerous to democracy" in [your books]. I believe strongly that the biggest danger to democracy is perpetrated by those who would dictate what people shall read, think, listen to or say. I am not alone among my fellow Americans in this belief, nor in my distress at the distrustful spirit the U.S. Government exhibits by actions such as this.

Mattituck, New York
I regard you as a fellow American, and that you were prevented from entering the U.S. fills me with shame and outrage. That any man's views and advocacies should be *feared* is antithetical to the whole concept of healthy democracy . . . that you, who have given so much to us, should be interdicted by some flunky carrying out a pin-headed policy was an insult to you and to all Americans. I apologize . . .

Fairbanks, Alaska
America is a very strong country? It does not possess the strength to allow Farley Mowat to penetrate its borders however . . . I hope you stick to your guns and not go to the immigration people and try and explain everything . . . The U.S. indeed acted just like we expect the Ruskies to do. Too bad for us!

Springfield, Ohio (postmark; no return address)

I am so glad you have decided to remain in Canada. I'm sure that is what your many admires [*sic*] prefer.

And as much as I love animals, I think there is a greater need to preserve the fast disappearing loyal American that believes you wouldn't have been denied admittance if you didn't deserve it. So just stay there in Canada and sulk.

P.S. We need you like you need another Quebec.

Eugene, Oregon

Please accept my apologies for the way you have been treated by the Immigration and Nazification Service. If we had had a more enlightened immigration policy from the beginning, the forbears of Alan Nelson, the Immigration Commissioner, would have been excluded.

Winchester, New Hampshire

The greatest embarrassment over this most recent gaffe by the Reagan administration is not just that it is wrongheaded and paranoid, but that it is so stupid and petty. By their actions you have been wronged – but we and they have been shamed.

Clawson, Michigan

I find it ironic that President Reagan will honour German soldiers on Sunday, May 5, while insulting a man who fought to keep fascism from spreading across the world.

Fort Kent, Maine

Congratulations to you on shaking your fist at our petty tyrants in Washington. You know, of course, that the embarrassing antics of our present regime do *not* reflect the attitudes of most Americans. I am proud of your stance and of what it must mean to Canadians.

Gloversville, New York

The citizens of America shall never forget the great service that the Canadian Embassy did to six Americans during the Iranian hostage crisis . . . unfortunately you are an ignominious disgrace to Canada and to democracy worldwide.

You must be an irrational madman to shoot at American jets . . . do you not realize the purpose of those brave men in those aircraft? They are there to protect Canada! By the way, the day the President of the United States apologizes to you is the day you crawl all the way to Washington, D.C. and kiss the floor of the Oval Office. This is the land of Abraham Lincoln; the land of the Declaration of Independence and the Liberty Bell; and the land of Hope and Freedom for all. I am glad you have not defiled it with your presence.

P.S. You know, you look just like Karl Marx.

Grand Haven, Michigan

It is a good thing the present administration was not in power [when our country was founded] or Tom Paine and others of his kind would not have been admitted. For a country that was founded on new thoughts and ideas, we have sure sunk a long way.

Santa Fé, New Mexico

I'm so mad that I went out this morning and bought all of your books . . . please know that the majority of people in the United States would welcome you with open arms.

Killingworth, Connecticut

A nation which made a hero out of a brutal butcher like "Buffalo Bill" looks damned silly drawing the line against an author like yourself.

Kankakee, Illinois

Now that you are a subversive I dread the appearance of the F.B.I. at my door. I have ten books written by you, two of them autographed. I drove up to Windsor, Ontario to get them autographed when you were signing there in November . . . Think of the charges against me: possession of subversive material; transportation of such across the border; corresponding with a known foreign subversive; and laughing at my Country's idea of subversion.

Clairton, Pennsylvania

I know this is too little and too late but I'd like to apologize for my country. It's beautiful, and a great place to live but unfortunately not perfect . . . I'd as soon suspect a moose of being too dangerous to let into the country as Farley Mowat.

Vancouver, Washington
I envy your happy position of becoming a mighty uncomfortable burr between bureaucracy's buttocks and a very hard saddle. I hope you make it a long, uncomfortable ride for them.

Finally, there is this letter from Knoxville, Tennessee, published in the *New York Times*.

Hail the Artist, Ban the Artist
I was astounded that the INS had barred [Mowat] from entering the United States . . . (*NYT* news story, April 24).

In the same issue I read President Reagan's remarks at a National Medal of Arts ceremony . . . He contended that in closed societies artists are sometimes willing to be provocative and unpopular, but that their fate is often unenviable. Where there is liberty, he said, art succeeds. In open societies, he said, art flourishes . . .

The President's remarks . . . are an admirable expression of commitment . . . But, in the context of Mr. Mowat's exclusion, they become a hypocrisy that demeans both the President and the American people.

Although the travels of my corporeal body during Monday and Tuesday of this week were limited to a couple of dog-walks along the beach, I nevertheless had the feeling that I had voyaged 10,000 miles and more through the byways of that peculiar nation lying just out of sight across the grey expanse of Lake Ontario.

I also was experiencing a growing sense of empathy with the people who inhabited it, so that when I went to bed on Tuesday night I was actually looking forward to the arrival of the mailman in the morning – to the letters he would bring, which would bear me on to new discoveries.

VII

Wednesday to Friday, May 1-3

Harry Collins will drive you to San Francisco Airport at 1:00 p.m.
Depart San Francisco 2:15 p.m. Alaska Airline #87.
Arrive Seattle/Tacoma 4:00 p.m.
You will be met by Ken Rose and driven to Four Seasons Olympic Hotel. Ken will be your escort in Seattle region. Your schedule will include:
Seattle Post-Intelligencer interview
Midday, KIRO-Radio
Midday Edition, KING-Radio
Northwest Afternoon, KOMO-TV
Seattle Times interview
Noon News, KIRO-Radio
Various bookstores, including an autographing at Heritage Bookshop.

According to my tour schedule, Wednesday was to have been a free day, requiring of me only that I get from San Francisco to Seattle. In fact, it turned out to be almost a free day in Port Hope. Apart from a call from Canadian Press in Washington, the incubus-machine stayed silent. Even friends did not intrude upon the blessed peace, most of them having given up trying to reach either Claire or me after being rebuffed for days by busy signals.

The mail remained enormous. Buried in Wednesday's collection was a story by Bogdan Kipling, a Canadian columnist based in Washington. It gave me food for thought.

"It's taken a while, but Americans are getting the joke in

the Farley Mowat affair. They're beinning to ridicule the law, the enforcers, the striped-pants brigade and everybody else connected with designating the Canadian author a 'threat to national security' and barring him from travel in the United States . . .
"Martha Johnson, owner of the Francis Scott Key Book Shop in Georgetown, D.C., chuckles at the silliness of it all. But there is a depressing aspect to it; she says 'the Mowat affair bears out the current theory that everything is subversive, including the animal kingdom' . . .
"Mowat said in a telephone conversation that . . . 'Sea of Slaughter' [is] hated by the anti-environmental lobby. That lobby – which, like defeat, has no acknowledged father, yet, like a hydra, has nine heads – is probably behind Mowat's travel ban.
"The man who has written about deer and wolves, owls and whales, Vikings and wars, has been in the United States a number of times in recent years.
" 'I just threw my kilt over me head,' he joked over the phone, while telling he had no problems crossing the border as recently as five years ago. But since 'Sea of Slaughter', published last year in Canada, 'they lowered the boom'.
"Oddly enough the Canadian Embassy here is not very curious what lurks behind Mowat's name on the INS 'lookout book' of undesirables: 'I'm not even sure whether we bothered to double-check on speculations that . . . firing of a .22 rifle at an American B-52 nuclear bomber . . . got him on the black list,' Embassy spokesman John Fielding said. Nor does the Embassy seem to have asked the date of Mowat's proscription. And perhaps just as well . . . INS spokesman Duke Austin told me 'a lot of information was furnished to the United States by the Canadian government . . .'
"Asked directly whether the Mounties 'fingered' Mowat, Austin replied: 'That could very possibly be, but I will not say this.' He added: 'The RCMP and other organizations in Canada identified people who had certain affiliations.'
"Talking all this time about Mowat and nobody else, Austin emphasized 'there are various exchanges of information, and always have been, between the Canadian and the U.S. governments'.

"If the Mounties thought that Mowat's concern for our common habitat was subversive, that's not an excuse for Americans. But then strange things happen in Reagan's land."

In the hurly-burly of trying to cope with the demands of the media, I had not had time to consider some disquieting suspicions about the role External Affairs might have played in the affair. Now I had time. And Kipling's column, together with a letter from Ottawa, encouraged speculation.

Driven into a corner, both the U.S. State Department and the INS had strongly implied that their action in barring me had been the result of some form of collaboration between them and the Canadian authorities. Yet the RCMP would not have been involved at any time later than May of 1980, when their "information service" to the INS was terminated by the then Solicitor General of Canada, Robert Kaplan. However, if the information contained in a letter I had also just received was credible, my fall from grace took place well after that date.

This letter was a stunner. It was written by an admirer of my work who was in a position to know whereof he spoke. The essence of it was contained in one pregnant paragraph.

"You should be advised that External probably knew in advance that you would not be permitted to cross the border . . . a high level decision had been taken that the allegations you made against some departments [of the Canadian government] in your book *Sea of Slaughter* were to be resisted as far as their propagation was concerned."

If this meant what it appeared to mean, then it seemed likely that I had been given the gears by my own government, not just in the past by the RCMP but in the here and now. During subsequent days I was to spend a good deal of time considering this unpalatable possibility.

There was, first of all, the question of why External Affairs had so abruptly abandoned the West Coast tour, *which was its own brainchild*. The reason given – that all three West Coast consulates had unexpectedly found themselves too busy to deal with it – no longer seemed plausible.

A secondary explanation was advanced at a later date: because I had gone to Australia in March under External's sponsorship, the Department would have had trouble justifying the cost of another sponsored trip in the same year. This did not wash either. An officer of the cultural section of External in Ottawa called me in early May to ask if I would like to represent Canadian writers at a June literary conference in West Germany – all expenses paid, of course.

On Wednesday afternoon, May 1st, I made a call to the lady at the Canadian Writers' Union who had been commissioned by External to organize my West Coast tour. I inquired whether she had kept a record of what had taken place. When she said yes, I asked for it.

It was most illuminating.

By February 27th, the tour organizer for the Writers' Union had made all the main arrangements and required only operational confirmation from the Canadian Consulates in Los Angeles, San Francisco, and Seattle. However, she was unable to reach *any* of the cultural attachés by telephone, even after several attempts. Messages asking these people to call her back brought no response. She then dispatched special delivery letters asking for confirmation of the arrangements. There were no replies.

It was not until March 6th that she finally reached Allan Unger at the Consulate in San Francisco – the man who had originated the request to External in Ottawa that I be invited to make the tour. Unger's enthusiasm had evidently cooled. There might be a problem, he said, "regarding [Mowat's] environmental views." He did not elaborate; nor would he confirm that the tour would go ahead as planned.

On March 18th, still without any response from the other two Consulates, by dint of great persistence, the organizer reached Simone Auger at the Los Angeles Consulate. Ms. Auger was evasive. The Consulate, she said, was going to be very busy in April, and perhaps the Mowat tour should be postponed until the fall.

Growing somewhat desperate by now, and finding the whole situation inexplicable, the organizer again called Unger. He now told her that *all* the Consulates would be very busy until autumn and would prefer Mowat to postpone the tour. He gave no indication of the nature of the activities that would so preoccupy the Consulates. Nor did he remark on the fact that my tour called for almost no involvement by consular staff, since all arrangements had been made by the Writers' Union in conjunction with the publicity department of Atlantic Monthly Press.

On March 19th the organizer reached Louise Hubbard at the San Francisco Consulate and was told that "April is not convenient for a Mowat tour." The following day an apologetic cultural officer in Ottawa finally called – to say that, "without the Consulates' assistance, it would seem advisable to postpone the tour." And that was that.

The message log concludes with the laconic comment: "At no time was any written reply received from any of the Consulates." Nothing in writing.

What the Writers' Union *did* receive was a frantic letter from Michael Bauman reporting that External Affairs had cancelled my visit to the university and offering to pay the costs of bringing me to Chico. Asked later what explanation he had been given for the cancellation, Bauman was clearly embarrassed. "I'd rather not discuss it. You see, we depend heavily on the co-operation of the Consulates for our Canadian Studies program." Perhaps he would have told me more if I had pressed him, but I did not feel justified in doing so. Furthermore, I thought I already knew the reason.

I have good and loyal friends in the news business, and one of them undertook a small investigation on my behalf in that moose-muskeg-of-the-mind called Ottawa. He reported:

"There's no hard and fast proof – seldom is for stuff like this – but I hear External was tipped off by the good buddies in Washington there was going to be trouble when you tried to cross the border. They knew when, and where, that was going to be.* The word is that some people didn't want you peddling your subversive ideas about conservation in the U.S.A. . . . If you're feeling paranoid, don't apologize. I'd say you had some reason."

Paranoid? No, sir! That is a state of mind that I eschew – although I must admit it isn't always easy.

---

* The Writers' Union organizer had, of course, submitted my proposed schedule to External. My departure date and place remained unchanged when Atlantic Monthly Press took over the tour arrangements.

Since I was not able to be in Seattle on Thursday, Seattle came to me. To start the day, I was interviewed by the *Seattle Post-Intelligencer*, which not only ran a long news account about my difficulties but an editorial as well.

"Twice in the last week the federal government denied entry into the United States to prominent foreigners.

"Who are these suspicious characters? Terrorists? Criminals? Spies?

"No. One is a writer-naturalist, the other a poet-priest.

"Farley Mowat . . . was stopped as he boarded a California-bound plane in Toronto . . . [Nicaraguan] Ernesto Cardenal, Roman Catholic priest and noted poet . . . was refused a U.S. visa for a speaking tour of several campuses . . .

"What nonsense. Such individuals should not be barred from our borders regardless of their political views. This is not the Soviet Union. They're spouting ideas, not bullets. Denying them entry is, well, un-American."

The *Seattle Times* was next and subsequently ran a feature piece putting me on record as saying, "We can't prove it yet, but people who have been doing some digging say it looks like the gun lobby is deeply involved." My suspicion – that the real reason External Affairs had cancelled out of the tour was because of pressure from the anti-environmentalists – was also reported. When the *Times* writer asked the Canadian Consulate in Seattle to comment on this, a spokesman admitted (with surprising candour), "It was one of our considerations."

At 4:00 p.m., a very determined woman interviewer from KGMI-Radio in Bellingham got me on the air and refused to relinquish her grip until a producer from KING-Radio, in Seattle itself, somehow persuaded a telephone operator to cut in on the line so that I could do an interview for his station. That evening, I spent an hour on the air with Joel Spivak of KNBR-Radio in San Francisco.

By Friday, things eased off again. The highlight of this day was a panel discussion on the McCarran-Walter Act, conducted by the British Broadcasting Corporation from Glasgow. I shared the spotlight with Larry Adler, famed harmonica player and a charter member of the Excludees Club.

A spokesman for the U.S. Embassy in London failed to materialize, either in the flesh or via telephone.

Seattle apart, interest in the story continued to shift away from my personal involvement and to focus on the larger issue, as witness this account from the Canadian Press bureau in Washington.

"Author Farley Mowat's run-in with U.S. immigration officials over his aborted visit to the United States has injected new life into a smouldering debate over a law rooted in the anti-Communist hysteria of the McCarthy era.

"The 1952 law, which gives the U.S. government broad authority to deny entry to foreigners for reasons of 'national security', was approved after Congress rallied behind Senator Pat McCarran's call for a new immigration law because 'criminals, Communists and subversives are now gaining admission to this country like water through a sieve'.

"Then-president Harry Truman was disgusted.

" 'Seldom has a bill exhibited the distrust evident here for citizens and aliens alike,' he said in his veto message. But his veto was subsequently overturned by a Congress spooked by allegations that Communists had infiltrated all aspects of American society, ranging from government to Hollywood's movie industry.

"The Immigration and Nationality Act, also known as the McCarran-Walter Act, has been controversial ever since. Attempts to rewrite it have gone nowhere, despite admissions from various administrations, including the Reagan team, that it needs amendment.

"Democratic congressman Barney Frank of Massachusetts will try again next week when he introduces a bill in the House of Representatives aimed at stripping the law of provisions that deny entry to foreigners because of their political beliefs . . .

"Joe Rauth, a leading U.S. civil rights lawyer, says he was shocked by Mowat's treatment. 'It's really ridiculous,' he said Thursday in an interview. 'The Statue of Liberty doesn't mean very much when people are acting that way.'

"American playwright Arthur Miller . . . calls the law 'garbage' left over from the McCarthy era . . .

"Civil rights activists alternately brand it as embarrassing, antiquated, hypocritical and a cynical betrayal of proclaimed adherence to the U.S. Constitution's first amendment, guaranteeing free speech. The irreverent Mowat uses less publishable words to describe the law and U.S. immigration authorities . . .

"Other prominent Canadians have come up against the same law including Manitoba Attorney General Roland Penner . . . and writer George Woodcock . . . Former prime minister Pierre Trudeau also is believed to have been on the list briefly in the early 1950s . . .

"Morton Halperin, director of the Washington-based Centre for National Security Studies, and a leading advocate of amending the law, said Mowat's case has rejuvenated the debate. It has reminded people that the law is outdated, and produced another round of needed editorials on the subject."

The number of Canadians who have been excluded from the United States under the McCarran Act is unknown, but it *is* reported from unofficial U.S. sources that at least 3,000 are named in the "lookout book," and it *is* known that hundreds of Canadians are turned back at the U.S. border every year for whatever reasons. Searching out the stories of those victimized by the McCarran Act is difficult because so many excludees are fearful of being besmirched by the McCarthy-Communist brush, and so are unwilling to talk.

In 1984, Stephan Phizicky, a producer for the prestigious CBC public affairs television program, *The Journal*, made a two-part documentary on the subject. It was called "Blacklist." Phizicky tracked down more than a hundred excludees but could find only seven willing to appear on the program, and even some of them sought anonymity. Those who refused to take part cited fear for their jobs, fear of the hostility of neighbours who might assume that, because the U.S. government had rejected them, they must be people of dubious repute, and fear of further antagonizing U.S. authorities who might some day – they hoped – relent and let them enter Eden.

It is important to note that a great many of those on the INS blacklist are now people in their sixties and older who got on the list because of political activities, associations, or accusations dating back as far as half-a-century. Some were indeed members of the Communist Party during the terrible days of the "Dirty Thirties." Some grew up in families, one or more members of which were or *had* been Communists or Communist sympathizers. Many had come no closer to that fatal contamination than to attend a rally, a meeting, a youth conference, even a protest march with which Communists had some association.

In the case of renowned Canadian violinist Steven Staryk, one of those who did appear on "Blacklist," the crime consisted of playing his violin at ethnic youth gatherings when he himself was still a youth. One such occasion was a social evening attended by young people of Ukrainian extraction, sponsored by the Labour Progressive Party of Canada, which, be it noted, was a perfectly legal political party in Canada at that time.

Staryk did not suspect he had been blacklisted until he attempted to enter the U.S. in the 1960s while travelling with the Toronto Symphony Orchestra. Not only was Staryk, together with five other symphony musicians, refused entry, but all six were subsequently fired by the orchestra's management, presumably as a consequence of the INS's accusations against them.

Another victim who appeared on "Blacklist" was Dr. Barker Fairley, ninety-seven-year-old painter, literary figure, scholar, and one of Canada's revered intellectual icons.

Because his wife, now long since dead, was an avowed Communist, Fairley found himself blacklisted when, in the early 1960s, he attempted to cross the border *en route* to take up a post as visiting professor in that notorious den of left-wing iniquity, Bryn Mawr College. Although never a Communist himself, and despite many attempts by influential friends, admirers, and Canadian government officials to clear him, his name remains in the "lookout book," and he is still proscribed from entering the United States.

Another excludee who appeared on the program was Roland Penner, Attorney General of Manitoba. Penner grew up in a family that had espoused communism during the thirties and through the wartime period when Russia was being hailed in North America as our stalwart ally against the Nazis. Himself a member of the Party in his youth, Penner outgrew the association, as did so many other young people of his generation. Nevertheless, he landed on the blacklist and would certainly have remained there all his life had he not achieved high public office and, as a special concession by U.S. authorities, been granted a form of diplomatic immunity which now enables him to enter the United States.

Ordinary Canadian citizens cannot expect, nor can they usually obtain, such preferential treatment. One of the few ways open to them to gain admittance is a grotesquely demeaning procedure imposed by the INS that can, if one is lucky and willing to abase oneself, result in the granting of something called "Defector Status," which, once obtained, opens the doors to Paradise. However, to obtain this benison one must submit to months of interrogation by the INS, during which the events and associations of one's whole lifetime are coldly scrutinized. The applicant is required to disavow all past actions and attitudes that could be construed as being sympathetic to communism; deny all concomitant friendships and associations; and not only declare but *prove* that he or she has become an *anti*-Communist and *has been* such for at least the five preceding years.

Proof that the recantation is no sham requires evidence such as the expression of anti-Communist sentiments in private letters and/or published writings, together with the testimony of friends, associates, and neighbours, to one's active anti-Communist stance. Evidence of *physical* opposition to communism is especially useful.

That is not all. The applicant must also be prepared to find five witnesses to his or her conversion who will *themselves* be willing to submit to interrogation and investigation in order to ensure that *they* are free of any latent Communist tendencies or sympathies.

It is small wonder that so few of those who find themselves in the tar pit called the "lookout book" ever manage to escape from that morass. It is small wonder that many people who have investigated the blacklist and the McCarran-Walter Act are convinced that both are maintained in force not so much to protect America from Communist subversion but as a way of pressuring foreigners into behaving according to the approved tenets of the U.S. government.

"There is no doubt in my mind," a highly placed Canadian legal official told me, "that it is used in a singularly vicious manner to keep people who are critical of the U.S.A., especially from Canada and the Latin American countries, in line. It's the old carrot and the whip. If you don't say bad things about them, you can come and visit their lovely garden and enjoy the fruits therein. If you speak ill of them, they'll shut you out."

Black book, blacklist . . . blackmail.

One of the many prominent Canadians who stepped out of line, and felt the whip in consequence, was Pierre Elliott Trudeau, Prime Minister of Canada from 1968 to 1984, except for one brief interruption. In his youth, Trudeau was a free-thinker with a restless curiosity and was afflicted with few dogmatic preconceptions. As a founder of and major contributor to the Montreal magazine *Cité libre*, he not only showed left-wing sympathies but upon occasion was downright critical of U.S. foreign policies. In his support of the grim struggle of Quebec asbestos workers to gain just treatment from the American-owned Johns-Manville Company, he demonstrated praiseworthy concern for the lot of the underdog. In his peregrinations around the world, including a walking tour in Red China in the early fifties and participation in an economic conference in Moscow in 1952, he demonstrated tolerance of and curiosity about political systems whose philosophies conflicted with those of North American capitalism.

Then, one day in 1954, Trudeau discovered there was a price to pay for this independence of thought and action. *En route* to New York in his own car, he was stopped at the Quebec/Vermont border and told by an INS officer that he could not proceed. Genuinely puzzled, he asked for an explanation. He was given none. This annoyed him, but did not make him really angry since he knew that if he jogged north, then east, then south again, he would find a border post on a minor road where he would probably be passed through with no more than the usual superficial questions. "You a Canadian?" Yes. "Where you going?" New York. "Staying long?" Just for the weekend. "Okay, buddy, on your way."

When he returned to Montreal he did not pursue the matter, having assessed it as a minor bureaucratic aberration. However, in 1956 he was invited to attend a Commonwealth Conference in London. Since this would involve "transiting" through the United States, he thought it would be as well to affirm that his 1952 experience at the border had been of no consequence. He called the U.S. Consulate in Montreal. Only then did he learn that he was in the "lookout book" and permanently barred from the U.S.A.

This was a situation which, for personal reasons, he could not afford to accept and so, to use his own word for it, he made arrangements with the U.S. authorities to "whiten" himself. After submitting to the investigative process, which included such indignities as being fingerprinted like a common criminal, he was eventually given clearance. The details of what he had to undergo, or of how he successfully achieved what hundreds of other Canadians have failed to achieve, remain unknown. It *is* known, however, that it took him a year to manage it. And to this day, he still does not know what it was that put him on the blacklist. His own best guess is that it was his criticisms of the U.S.A. in *Cité libre*.

Trudeau was luckier than George Woodcock. Woodcock is known to most literate Canadians as a first-rate writer possessed of an incisive mind, whose commentaries on the human condition are calculated to slip between the ribs with the swiftness and accuracy of a stiletto. He is not admired by some members of the Canadian establishment, but he appeals to those who cannot abide cant, subterfuge, and intellectual dishonesty. He may not be well known to Americans in general – but he certainly *is* to the INS.

He tells his story in the September 27, 1984, issue of *The New York Review of Books*, from which with his permission I have excerpted the following passages:

"Last Christmas Eve [1983] my wife and I set out from Vancouver for Sydney, Australia. At 11:30 p.m. the plane put down at Honolulu airport, where we intended to break the flight . . . Shuffling forward to the immigration desk, I saw the woman officer was working with a black book – a literal black book, heavy and thick . . . When the woman took my passport and flicked the book to W, the smile she wore for tourists stiffened . . . An attendant took our passports into an inner office where I saw a man glance at them, and wander away. A little later, he called us into his room . . .

" 'Mr. Woodcock,' he said . . . 'I have to inform you that you are inadmissible into the United States of America.' I knew immediately what distant ghost had unexpectedly returned, but I still asked why. 'You're in the lookout book. I can't tell you why.' . . .

"The Qantas agent appeared saying he had another plane leaving for Sydney in an hour . . . and at one o'clock on Christmas morning we resumed our journey. As we flew southward through the night, I remembered with a vividness I had not experienced for a quarter of a century, the long-ago events that had led, almost on the very eve of Nineteen Eighty-Four, to my being treated as something near a criminal . . ."

Woodcock began his writing career in England during the grim years of the 1930s. Like Graham Greene, George Orwell, and many other contemporaries, he was for a time enamoured of the far left. However, "hating fascism, but fearing Stalinism just as much . . . rejecting violence, whether of the state or of the revolution," he became a philosophical anarchist. By 1949, when he came to Canada, he had no remaining political involvements. In 1951, he won a Guggenheim Fellowship and spent six months studying and writing in California.

In 1954, he was offered a visiting professorship at the University of Washington but, by then, the McCarthy-induced witch hunt was sweeping the United States. When Woodcock applied to the U.S. consul in Vancouver for a residence visa, he was told that, because of his anarchist background, he could no longer enter the United States under any circumstance.

"The [McCarran-Walter] Act declares that anyone who is – or has been, no matter how long ago – an anarchist is inadmissible . . . Merely to have declared oneself an anarchist at any time in one's life is grounds enough for exclusion

. . . Henry David Thoreau, if he were an alien, could be excluded on the strength of his essay, 'Civil Disobedience' . . .

"The University of Washington . . . sent an emissary to Vancouver to reason with the consul. He came to me and reported: 'You might be let in if you were willing to say, I'm not an anarchist anymore *and* I deeply regret I ever was one.' It sounded too much like the recantation formula of the Holy Inquisition for my taste . . .

"During the 1970s I began to test the American border. I crossed regularly and freely. I flew into the U.S. and passed airport checks without trouble. And then, last Christmas, after twenty-eight years, my name turned up again, in the Honolulu black book. Why was it there and not on the computers at other places? Have old lists, under Reagan, been revived and redistributed?* . . .

"There is no automatic process by which the black book is revised. Names presumably stay on the list even after their owners die. Getting off the list requires either an act of Congress, as happened with Arthur Koestler, who had been a Communist during the Thirties, or an application for defector status (amounting to a recantation), which nonetheless is difficult to obtain. Otherwise, exclusion can be waived only in special cases for specified periods of time. This too is a cumbersome legal process, involving a great deal of grovelling, and has no guarantee of success.

"Only a change in the law can deal with the situation . . . Representative Barney Frank has introduced a bill, HR 5227,** with this intent . . . Perhaps at last the need for the tedious waiver procedure, which many of us find too humiliating to pursue, will be brought to an end and American and foreign writers and intellectuals will once again mingle freely without discrimination for ideological reasons."

---

* I have made my own investigation of this. It appears that, during the latter part of the sixties and through the seventies, the "lookout book" had, sensibly, fallen into general disuse. It seems to have been rehabilitated in the early years of the Reagan regime. My own case argues for the accuracy of this assessment since, as recently as 1979, I was able to enter the U.S. without difficulty.

** Which did not pass, but which Frank has revised and re-introduced.

VIII
Saturday, May 4

Ken Rose will arrange a limo to pick you up at your hotel at 7:30 a.m.
Depart Seattle/Tacoma 9:35 a.m. American #24.
Arrive Toronto 6:45 p.m.

"It's marvelous to be back home," I told my wife happily as I poured the wine for dinner. "Damn glad it's over, though. Wouldn't want to go through *that* again!"

The roast was still sizzling as Claire brought it to the table. "I don't see why not. Maybe you should do all your promo tours this way. Think of the advantages: home cooking, and no jet lag . . . somebody to make sure you change your socks . . . and think of the money you save your publishers! They might raise your royalties in gratitude."

"Fat bloody chance! More likely to cut 'em . . ." I sliced viciously into the joint to demonstrate my meaning. "But this is a night to celebrate. Let's drink to those kind souls who arranged my impossible journey." I put down the carving tools and raised my glass. "To Benedict Ferro and the INS – not to forget the U.S. State Department; Senator Pat McCarran, wherever he may be; the RCMP; and our very own cement-heads in Ottawa . . . Peace be on them all as, I trust, it now will be on us!"

And peace did finally descend upon our house. Although in the days ahead echoes of war still rumbled on the far horizon, I was well out of the combat zone. Exhausted, but secure of life and limb, I observed what followed almost with detachment.

Some big guns continued firing.

Time contributed a two-column salvo – "An Author's Forbidden Passage" – in which the American Civil Liberties Union was quoted on the obvious: "There has been a significant increase under this Administration of overtly political expulsions."

U.S.A. Today devoted an entire editorial page to the question of whether or not foreigners such as myself, holding views to which the U.S. government was opposed, should be allowed into the United States. The editors and most of the contributors to the page agreed that such people *should* be allowed in.

Secretary of State George Shultz equivocated in fine cementhead fashion: "As a general proposition I think we have to favor free speech, but it can get abused by people who do not wish us well."

A sixty-year-old woman with the evocative name of Gin Rich (she is a corporate secretary from Hurst, Texas, who wears a ten-gallon hat to prove it) said: "I'm in favor of restricting visitors to the United States who speak against our country. If they want to speak to people about communism or if they want to speak ill of the United States, let them do it in their own country. Our young people are too easily influenced. The last thing they need is another negative influence."

I made my own contribution to the page with a guest column written in the heat of battle some days earlier: "If I'm a Threat, You're Really in Trouble." It ended on this note:

"Up here in Canada we're talking about the Paper Curtain surrounding the U.S.A. It's a curtain intended to exclude ideas and idea-bearers that are anathema to the U.S. administration.

"Your Bill of Rights bars the authorities from banning books, but they've found a way to prevent people like myself from propagating a book's contents. It's very frightening – not for me personally – but it bodes ill for your country. It amounts to a form of state censorship, pure and simple."

And then there was Senator Paul Simon (D., Illinois) who read into the Congressional Record a piece by *Chicago Tribune* editor and columnist Stephen Chapman. Here are some excerpts from it.

"To the ramparts men! Mothers, lock up your daughters! Farley Mowat's on his way! This infamous Canadian writer has been denied entrance to the United States by a vigilant

118

sentinel guarding our border, but the cowardly Reagan administration faced with complaints from the Canadian government, lamely decided on appeasement . . .

"[Mowat] was denied entry under a McCarthy-era law . . . [which] tries to isolate Americans from anyone who is not normal in every way – the mentally retarded, the insane, or formerly insane, sexual deviates, drug addicts, alcoholics, beggars, prostitutes and the ever-present polygamists.

"That's just for starters. The law disinvites foreigners with unacceptable political views . . . [including] those advocating 'opposition to all organized government' . . . [a clause] which would keep out some of my fellow libertarians who don't even like the disorganized kind. In case we've missed anyone, those of you contemplating activities 'prejudicial to the public interest' can also get lost.

"All this would be funny if it did not have the full power of the U.S. government behind it . . . The authors of this law, and the people enforcing it, obviously regard ideas as communicable diseases . . . but unlike measles germs, ideas have other means of transmission, like books. As the law stands, the U.S. government can't ban Gabriel Garcia Marquez's writings . . . doing so would violate the First Amendment. It can't even prevent him personally arguing his case for American ears since he can do that via telephone, tape recordings or broadcast transmission. All it can do is keep his body from crossing the border. What on earth does that accomplish, except making the INS a fit subject for ridicule?

"It would make sense to keep Mowat out if there was any evidence that he is dangerous to the U.S. government or anyone else. But there isn't. The political exclusions in the law serve only to punish people for having wrong opinions. If we're going to do that, let's start with the people who enacted it."

The final rumble, insofar as this book is concerned, comes from a Pittsburgh newspaper in an editorial called "The Treatment of Mowat."

"Never mind that Americans holding [extreme] views on the left or right are free to espouse their ideologies at home, even run for office . . . they're protected by the First Amendment . . .

"Shouldn't foreign visitors have the same protection? Of course they should. Sensibly, U.S. Rep. Barney Frank, D-Mass., proposes amendments to the McCarran-Walter Act that would repeal the broad-brush exclusionary provisions . . . That way Americans could sift and winnow divergent opinions for themselves, as the framers of the Constitution intended.

"Recently President Reagan saluted the tradition of free inquiry in a different context. 'In an atmosphere of liberty,' Reagan said in an eloquent speech to winners of the National Medal of Arts, 'artists and patrons are free to think the unthinkable and create the audacious; they are free to make both horrendous mistakes and glorious celebrations.'

"Let the government now practise what the president (and the Constitution) preaches – and welcome the expression of Farley Mowat's unthinkable, audacious ideas, whatever they are."

I had trouble getting to sleep on the night of my "homecoming." My mind was a wheeling kaleidoscope of too many impressions from the hectic days just past.

There was the shock and outrage of the first day – the fears and apprehensions as battle was joined, the enormous relief as unexpected allies rallied to my side, the heady excitement of the war of words that followed, and the exhilaration of seeing the cementheads finally take cover.

I needed a soporific, so I padded down to the kitchen for a glass of rum mixed with warm milk – a sovereign family remedy that soon began to do its work. I was just drifting off when, shatteringly, the telephone began to shrill. In a mood more fit for killing than for kindly words, I stumbled to it. An unctuous voice slithered into my ear.

"Well, hi there Mr. Mowat. Listen, I'm a tour-boat operator in San Diego. We hear you're crazy about whales. Well, so are we! And we've got a cruise coming up to scout the grey whales migrating north. Wondered would you like to come along? Our rates are awful easy on the wallet . . ."

"*Another* interview?" Claire asked crossly as I slumped back into bed beside her.

"No, dear. Just a routine call this time. Life's back to normal now. Good night . . . sleep tight."

My story logically stops here – but one thing remains to be added. I began this book with Michael Bauman, so I shall end it with this letter to him.

Dear Michael:
Once again let me say how sorry I am that I failed to make it down to Chico. Please pass on my heartfelt thanks to all the good people there – students, teachers, townsfolk and the 'dwellers in the hills' who rallied so vigorously to my support.

Tell them that, not only do I feel no pain as a result of what the I.N.S. did, I think I owe the sods a debt of gratitude. No, not because they provided so much publicity for my book when their intention was to do the opposite, but for quite another reason.

You see, if they hadn't blocked me from entering your country I might never have embarked upon the personal discovery of an America I never knew.

Like many of us 'aliens' I nurtured the conviction that the *image* of the U.S.A. so assiduously projected by your various establishments was one with the reality.

I believed that the bullying, arrogant, astonishingly insensitive way your political, commercial and military leaders routinely regard, and all too often treat those of us who live outside the Pale, was a fair reflection of the attitudes of the American people as a whole – even of that portion which ought to have been smart enough to know better.

I believed that most of you supported, even if you did not necessarily glory in, the bellicose posturing of those New Romans of yours who seem to be pursuing their dreams of Empire as fervently as the Soviets. I believed that most of you were truly convinced by your own propaganda that the Imperial Eagle had a God-given right, if not a bounden duty, to impose its will upon 'the lesser breeds'.

I have held to these beliefs through most of my adult life. Now I'm not so sure.

I'm beginning to think – hope, would be a better word – that the image may be false.

Where did I find the grounds for doubting my long-held convictions? I found them in the support given to me during my hassle with your government by Americans from many walks of life and from almost every state in the Union. And, *especially* I found them in the impassioned rejection by so many of you of the authoritarian, undemocratic, and frequently underhanded procedures employed against all of us 'excludees' by those who are supposed to serve, and do your will.

In short, I found my grounds for doubting the validity of the image as a consequence of an incredible journey into the minds and hearts of your compatriots.

And so I begin to hope that Americans may yet demonstrate the integrity and determination required to rediscover and refurbish the verities which were the birthright of your nation – those brave and humane truths your founders bequeathed to you, and on which your forbears based their faith in the evolution of a better world.

You ask what the odds are that I will get to visit you. I cannot tell. But, certainly, I'd dearly love to come . . . and so bring to full circle the discovery which properly began when you first wrote to me from Chico.

Hasta la vista!

Farley

A Postscript

The time-sense of governmental officials runs on a clock set to near-eternal slowness. On May 28th, when I had retired to my rural retreat in Cape Breton Island to write this book, I finally received a telephone call from Benedict Ferro. He was extremely affable, saying he was eager to "get together" with me to discuss my "application for information." He even sounded hopeful of a visit to my home, but I said "We might not let you in."

He sounded very indefinite about the information in my file and repeated his wish to discuss it face to face, but I said I would be in my remote retreat until the autumn, at which he agreed to send me "some material." Some additional material in the INS file, he said, could not be made available to me under the terms of the Freedom of Information Act; but Ferro said he would apply on my behalf for access to those materials.

The "file," which arrived a few days later, contained eight items, the most recent of which was dated 1968. I will briefly describe each item, in chronological order.

1. A newsclipping from *The Workers' Vanguard*, Toronto, Ontario, February 28, 1961, headlined "NTL FAIR PLAY FOR CUBA CMTTEE [*sic*] LAUNCHED AT TORONTO MASS RALLY." The article, about 600 words long, began: "The Fair Play for Cuba Committee launched in Toronto last month took a giant step forward with a mass meeting held in the First Unitarian Congregation on February 19th. Almost 400 turned out to hear guest speaker, Samuel Shapiro, professor of history at Michigan State University, and a well-known writer on Latin American affairs, speak on Perspectives for Cuba." Farther down the first column, it reads: "Now Farley Mowat, one of Canada's best known and most controversial

and stimulating writers, has joined the committee, along with [here follows a list of four journalists and politicians]."

2. A mimeographed newsletter of the Fair Play for Cuba Committee, dated April 8, 1961 – less than two weeks before the fated Bay of Pigs invasion by the CIA. It quotes "a report by Tad Szulc, of the *New York Times*, . . . which was headed 'U.S. helps Train Anti-Castro Army on Louisiana Soil' " and it goes on to say: "When Cuba's foreign minister, Raul Roa, laid charges in the United Nations, . . . that the U.S. was planning an invasion his country [*sic*], U.S. delegate Wadsworth condescendingly dismissed the charges as 'rubbish'." The newsletter carried my name, along with fourteen others, at its head.

3. A newsclipping from *Pacific Tribune*, dated February 1, 1963, headlined "Mowat Turns to Newfoundland" and ending with a paragraph next to which the INS had affixed some sort of official stamp. "Mowat's concern for his fellow man doesn't stop at minority groups; he has been active for some time now in the Canadian Campaign for Nuclear Disarmament."

4. A list of sponsors ("partial list") of the "Student Union for Peace Action" dated simply 1965, and containing, along with mine, twenty-two other names including those of Bertrand Russell, J.B. Priestly (misspelled), A.J.P. Taylor, and Linus Pauling.

5. The August-September, 1966, mimeographed Bulletin of Canadian Aid for Vietnam Civilians, Vancouver, B.C., bearing my name and twenty-two others on its letterhead. It stated that the chairman, Dr. Alan Inglis, left late in August for a tour to the U.S.S.R. "to meet several world famed personalities who are active in seeking peace in Vietnam." The group stated it was halfway to its goal of $20,000 for Vietnam Civilian Aid and went on: "It has come to our attention that a number of friends question the advisability of knitting woollen garments for the babies of Vietnam. May we assure volunteers and others that despite the tropical climate, nights are often cool, particularly in rainy seasons, and in mountainous areas."

6. A clipping from *Canadian Tribune*, Toronto, Ontario, issue of November 13, 1967. In part it reads: "Five hundred

people attended a concert meeting Oct. 26 celebrating the 50th anniversary of the October Revolution sponsored by the Canada USSR Association in Toronto's Westbury Hotel. The meeting was addressed by USSR Ambassador Ivan Schpedko, Stanley Ryerson, Editor of Horizons, and also heard a few words of greeting from author Farley Mowat who has just recently returned from the Soviet Union."

7. A clipping from *Ukrainian Canadian*, Toronto, Ontario, issue of December 15, 1967. It showed, under the heading "A Distinguished Visitor to Our Press," a group of people, not including me, gathered around "Chukchi writer Yuri Rytkheu, a representative of a far north minority group of some 12,000 people." The caption went on to say, "The writer was a guest of Canadian writer Farley Mowat who recently returned to Canada from a 12,000 mile trip across Siberia. He was accompanied by Rytkheu on this journey and in return invited him to visit Canada's far north."

8. Finally, in its entirety, this clipping from the *Ottawa Citizen*, Ottawa, Ontario, issue of March 22, 1968. *Wednesdaze [sic]*:

Author Farley Mowat won't command the "Col. J. Sutherland Brown Volunteer Brigade". The unit is to be organized June 29 at Moose Mountain Park, Sask. Its purpose is to "defend Canada against attacks from the U.S. Strategic Air Command". Brigade headquarters at Oxbow, Sask., says U.S. planes are carrying out simulated bombing attacks, at 500-foot levels, every 15 minutes, over the Prairies, with Canadian government sanction!

Mowat, who admits to firing at SAC planes carrying hydrogen bombs with a .22 calibre rifle from his Newfie backyard, had declined command of the Volunteers because they will use only blanks to repel the invaders. "I'd insist upon live ammo," he says. "These flights over Canada constitute de facto invasion – even if the yellowbellies in Ottawa have opened our borders to them.

"After all, we fought the Yanks in 1812 and kicked them the hell out of our country – but not with blanks."